Innkeepers' Best

Muffins

60 Delicious Recipes Shared by
Bed & Breakfast Innkeepers
Across the Country

Laura Zahn

Down to Earth Publications

Published by
Down to Earth Publications
1032 West Montana Avenue
St. Paul, MN 55117

Library of Congress Cataloging in Publication Data

Zahn, Laura C., 1957-
    Innkeepers' best muffins / Laura C. Zahn.
        p.   cm.
    Includes index.
    ISBN 0-939301-96-2
    1. Breakfasts 2. Muffins 3. Breads 4. Bed and breakfast accommodations—U.S.—directories.
    TX770.M83

Dewey System - Ideas and Recipes for Breakfast and Brunch - 641.52

Printed in the USA
97 98 99 00 01 5 4 3 2 1

Cover photo of Double Chocolate Muffins (recipe page 61), courtesy of Rancho San Gregorio, San Gregorio, CA. Back cover photo courtesy of the Beazley House, Napa, California (recipes on pages 81 and 121). Many thanks to these inns — and the others — all who shared their delicious recipes and wonderful stories!

Cover and interior design by Helene C. J. Anderson, Stillwater, Minnesota.

To order additional copies by mail, send a check or money order for $12.95 each to Down to Earth Publications, 1032 W. Montana Ave., St. Paul, MN 55117 (includes shipping by 4th class mail). If you wish UPS delivery, send a check for $13.95 and include a street address (no P.O. boxes). To charge your order with a Visa or MasterCard, call 800-585-6211 or fax 612-488-7862.

Introduction

*M*mmm, muffins. It's a rare individual who'll turn down a warm muffin, fresh from the oven, as part of a wonderful breakfast. A muffin and some fruit may suffice as a good breakfast itself!

Breakfast, as we have been told over and over, is the most important meal of the day. But in this toaster-pastry society, working families have become too busy for full breakfasts together on busy mornings. Because of that, muffins have become more popular. They are quick (often five minutes to mix, 15 or 20 to bake). They are hearty and tastier than a piece of toast. And they are as satisfying as a yeast bread or roll, filling your house with a wonderful aroma as they bake, but made with only a fraction of the time and effort. No wonder whipping up a batch of muffins has become a much-appreciated morning task, if only occasionally.

At comfortable B&B inns around the country, guests rarely get a look inside the kitchen. But if they did, they would see that busy innkeepers are hustling about, trying to properly time the courses of a delicious breakfast, often rising earlier than the chickens to do so. Innkeepers can use time-saving, one or two-bowl recipes, too. And, most importantly, the innkeepers' muffins must be absolutely scrumptious, making guests' mouths water.

Who better to ask when seeking sixty marvelous muffin recipes than B&B innkeepers? And, lucky for us, they willingly complied with their time-tested, guest-tested favorites. Some of these recipes can be made ahead, and others reheat or freeze particularly well, for additional practicality. Some are healthy, some so decadent they can be served for a dessert. All of them get "ooohs" and "aaahs" from guests every time, the ones that repeat guests request, and the ones that innkeepers are most-often asked to write down so guests can try them at home.

From Almond to Zucchini Lemon, there are enough creative muffin recipes in this book to please even the most experienced "muffineer." Recipes may use regional favorites, such as fresh persimmons, or sport a Southwestern flavor, like Chili Cheese Corn Muffins. For those lucky enough to have elderberries nearby, there's even a recipe for those rather-rare berry muffins. But most of these sixty varieties of muffins can be made by anyone, anywhere, anytime.

And if the 12 or so muffins each recipe makes are too many for you and yours to enjoy right from the oven, surely you have grateful friends and neighbors who would love a share of the batch! So spread the wealth of "good eatin'" contained in these pages. Bring a B&B breakfast home to your house — and maybe someone else's, too! We'll all have a better day for it!

— *Laura Zahn*

CONTENTS

Muffin Recipes ■ 7 to 125

63 ■ Elderberry Muffins, *The Inn at Shallow Creek Farm, Orland, CA*
65 ■ Ginger Pear Muffins, *Salisbury House, Seattle, WA*
67 ■ Ginger Rhubarb Muffins, *The Woods House Bed & Breakfast, Ashland, OR*
69 ■ Glazed Lemon Blueberry Yogurt Muffins, *Wedgwood Inns, New Hope, PA*
71 ■ Glazed Raspberry Lime Muffins, *The Adams Hilborne, Chattanooga, TN*
73 ■ Grandmother's Strawberry Muffins, *The Lady Goodwood Bed & Breakfast, Stillwater, MN*
75 ■ Harvest Fruit Muffins, *Watch Hill, Center Harbor, NH*
77 ■ Jane's Double-Good Michigan Blueberry Muffins, *The Inn at Ludington, Ludington, MI*
79 ■ Key Lime Muffins, *Diantha's Garden Bed & Breakfast, Southampton, MA*
81 ■ Mandarin Orange Muffins, *The Beazley House Bed & Breakfast Inn, Napa, CA*
83 ■ Maplewood Nut Muffins, *The Inn at Maplewood Farm, Hillsborough, NH*
85 ■ Melba Muffins, *Good Medicine Lodge, Whitefish, MT*
87 ■ Morning Glory Muffins, *The Inn at the Round Barn Farm, Waitsfield, VT*
89 ■ Orange Chocolate Chip Muffins, *Red Shutters, York Beach, ME*
91 ■ Orange Marmalade Muffins, *Garth Woodside Mansion Bed & Breakfast Country Inn, Hannibal, MO*
93 ■ Orange Nut Muffins, *Inn at Gristmill Square, Warm Springs, VA*
95 ■ Orange Pumpkin Nut Muffins, *Allen House Victorian Inn, Amherst, MA*
97 ■ Ozark Persimmon Muffins, *Walnut Street Inn, Springfield, MO*
99 ■ Peach Cobbler Muffins, *Windyledge Bed & Breakfast, Hopkinton, NH*
101 ■ Peach of a Tomato Muffins, *Wild Swan Inn, Lewes, DE*
103 ■ Peanut Butter Bran Muffins, *Grant Corner Inn, Santa Fe, NM*
105 ■ Pear Almond Muffins, *L'Auberge Provençale, White Post, VA*
107 ■ Pineapple Cream Muffins, *The Lamplighter Bed & Breakfast, Ludington, MI*
109 ■ Pumpkin Apple Streusel Muffins, *Grünberg Haus Bed & Breakfast, Waterbury, VT*
111 ■ Pumpkin Spice Muffins, *Lord Mayor's Bed & Breakfast Inn, Long Beach, CA*
113 ■ Raisin Bran Muffins, *Thimbleberry Inn, Bayfield, WI*
115 ■ Raspberry Cornmeal Muffins, *The Woods House Bed & Breakfast, Ashland, OR*
117 ■ Rhubarb Pecan Muffins, *Just-N-Trails Country Inn, Sparta, WI*
119 ■ Spicy Peach Muffins, *Angel Arbor Bed & Breakfast Inn, Houston, TX*
121 ■ Strawberry Shortcake Muffins, *The Beazley House Bed & Breakfast Inn, Napa, CA*
123 ■ White Chocolate Muffins, *Old Rittenhouse Inn, Bayfield, WI*
125 ■ Zucchini Lemon Muffins, *Angel Arbor Bed & Breakfast Inn, Houston, TX*

The Lamplighter
Bed & Breakfast

*J*udy and Heinz Bertram and their cocker spaniel, Freddy, welcome recreational and business travelers to their Queen Anne-style home, which was built in 1895 by a local doctor as his home and office. After living for more than twenty years in Germany and traveling extensively throughout Europe, the Bertrams brought their collection of fine antiques and original paintings and lithographs to their Michigan B&B.

They purchased their "dream B&B" virtually overnight, Judy said. She and Heinz added a deck with a gazebo and a red brick patio and extensive landscaping so that summer guests can enjoy refreshments outside. Judy is a Michigan native and former administrator in the Department of Defense school system overseas, and Heinz, originally from Germany, is a retired U.S. Air Force officer.

Breakfast may be served on the patio, in the gazebo or in the formal dining room, depending on the season. Afterwards, guests might head off to swim in Lake Michigan, stroll along its miles of sandy beaches, walk to the lighthouse at the entrance to Ludington harbor, or shop for antiques. Guests find plenty of outdoor activities year 'round, including biking through Ludington State Park, rated one of the state's best, skiing on miles of groomed cross-country trails, or hiking or strolling along nature trails. Judy and Heinz are happy to help guests plan their itinerary to explore scenic Western Michigan.

The Lamplighter Bed & Breakfast
602 East Ludington Avenue
Ludington, MI 49431
Toll-free 800-301-9792
Fax 616-845-6070

Almond Muffins

Innkeeper Judy Bertram always has these muffins on hand. "Although I bake a lot of different muffins, I use this recipe the most — they are quick and easy, taste delicious, and freeze well." Makes 12 muffins.

  1 egg, beaten
 ¾ cup milk
 ⅓ cup oil
 ½ teaspoon almond extract
  2 cups flour
 ½ cup sugar
  3 tablespoons baking powder
 ¼ teaspoon nutmeg
 ¼ cinnamon
 ⅛ teaspoon salt
 ½ cup almonds, chopped

- Preheat oven to 400 degrees.
- Mix the beaten egg with the milk, oil, and almond extract.
- In a separate bowl, mix together flour, sugar, baking powder, nutmeg, cinnamon, salt, and chopped almonds.
- Add the egg mixture to the flour mixture, and mix just to combine.
- Bake for 10 to 15 minutes.

Park Row Bed & Breakfast

*N*ot many inns draw guests just because of the innkeeper's collection of cookbooks or the fact that the cookie jar is always full for raiding. But in this case, the innkeeper is Ann Burckhardt, a popular food writer for the *Star Tribune* of the Twin Cities. She aims to make breakfasts memorable for her guests, who read her writing for years before she "retired" into full-time innkeeping in 1995. They love to read in her cookbook "library" and enjoy, perhaps, Maple Chocolate Chip Cookies.

Ann opened St. Peter's first bed-and-breakfast in 1990, several years before retirement, as a new challenge. She commuted the 66 miles to the Twin Cities from this peaceful Minnesota River Valley town, home of Gustavus Adolphus College.

Her gingerbread-trimmed B&B is a Carpenter Gothic home, circa 1870. It immediately captivated her during her search for a B&B. It needed minimal renovation to be turned into a four-guestroom inn, which she decorated with antiques, queen-sized beds, and down comforters.

Park Row Bed & Breakfast
525 West Park Row
St. Peter, MN 56082
507-931-2495

Apple-Barb Muffins

A hefty, satisfying treat for breakfast or mid-morning. "I use rhubarb from six plants behind my garage/barn, but you could use commercially frozen rhubarb if you wished," said Innkeeper Ann Burckhardt. Makes 16 muffins.

- ½ cup sugar
- 2 teaspoons cinnamon
- 2 cups unbleached flour
- 1 cup whole-wheat flour
- 2 teaspoons cinnamon
- 2 teaspoons baking powder
- ½ teaspoon baking soda
- ½ teaspoon salt
- 2 eggs
- 1⅓ cups packed brown sugar
- 1⅓ cups applesauce
- ½ cup vegetable oil
- 1½ cups rhubarb, chopped

- Preheat oven to 350 degrees. Grease muffin cups.
- Mix ½ cup sugar with the first 2 teaspoons of cinnamon to make cinnamon sugar. Set aside.
- In a large mixing bowl, stir together the flour, whole-wheat flour, second 2 teaspoons of cinnamon, baking powder, baking soda, and salt. Make a well in the center of these dry ingredients.
- In a medium bowl, combine the eggs, brown sugar, applesauce, and oil. Pour the egg mixture into the flour mixture. Stir just until all the ingredients are moistened. The batter will be lumpy. Fold in the chopped rhubarb.
- Spoon batter into greased muffin cups, filling nearly full. Lightly sprinkle cinnamon sugar on top — it is not necessary to use all the cinnamon sugar.
- Bake muffins for 30 to 35 minutes. Serve warm with butter.

Apple Gate Bed & Breakfast

*S*easonal fresh fruit is always a part of breakfast at the Apple Gate, and that includes fresh berries from a neighbor's organic farm, as well as apples, of course. Because Apple Gate is located just across the street from a ninety-acre apple orchard, Innkeeper Dianne Legenhausen chose an apple motif to decorate the inn, including naming the four guestrooms after apple varieties. Even Dianne and Ken's one hundred-pound yellow lab, Mac, is named after the McIntosh apple (the cat, Jessie, however, was acquired before the inn and has no apple ties).

Before innkeeping, Dianne taught music to elementary-age children and Ken was a police officer specializing in emergency rescues. While they had many friends in Long Island, New York, where they lived and worked for many years, they decided to head for the Monadnock region of New Hampshire, said to be picture-perfect Currier and Ives country, for their second careers as innkeepers.

They found this 1832 Colonial home just two miles from downtown Peterborough. It offered spacious accommodations for guests, including a double parlor, where guests may enjoy a fire, the library or a TV and collection of videos. Peterborough is home to the Sharon Arts Center and the Legenhausen's bed-and-breakfast is just a few miles from the Temple Mountain and Windblown ski areas.

Apple Gate Bed & Breakfast
199 Upland Road
Peterborough, NH 03458
603-924-6543

Apple Carrot Cinnamon Muffins

"Since we are located across the road from a ninety-acre apple orchard, we like to serve at least one apple food at breakfast," writes Innkeeper Dianne Legenhausen. "We're always looking for new apple recipes. Of all the apple muffins we have served our guests during our five years as innkeepers, this wheat apple muffin recipe is the most requested." Makes 12 muffins.

  ⅓ cup butter, softened
  ¾ cup sugar
  1 egg
  ¾ cup buttermilk
  1½ apples, peeled, cored, and chopped
  1 carrot, grated
  ⅓ cup raisins, optional
  1 cup flour
  1 cup whole-wheat flour
  1 teaspoon baking soda
  1 teaspoon cinnamon
  ½ teaspoon salt

Topping
  3 tablespoons sugar
  1 teaspoon cinnamon

- Preheat oven to 400 degrees. Grease muffin cups.
- Beat together the butter and ¾ cup sugar until creamy. Add the egg, and beat well.
- Add the buttermilk all at once, and stir in chopped apple, grated carrots, and optional raisins.
- In a separate bowl, stir together the flour, whole-wheat flour, baking soda, 1 teaspoon of cinnamon, and salt. Combine the flour mixture with the butter mixture, and blend well. Let the batter rest for 5 minutes.
- Spoon the batter into greased muffin cups.
- To make the topping, mix together the 3 tablespoons of sugar with the remaining 1 teaspoon of cinnamon. Sprinkle the batter with the topping.
- Bake for about 20 minutes.

The Stout Trout Bed & Breakfast

*I*nnkeeper Kathleen Fredricks found this former fishing lodge, located on Gull Lake in the Hayward Lakes region, when she returned to her home state after living in California. The building, complete with paint-on-velvet Elvis, needed a year's worth of major work. She gutted it and set to work, keeping only the original plank floors, and creating four large guestrooms.

Guests dine downstairs in the great room overlooking Gull Lake. In the winter, the forty acres behind the bed-and-breakfast are popular with cross-country skiing guests. In the summer, guests can fish for bass out front, or trout fish, canoe or tube the Namekagon River, swim, or berry-pick nearby. The bed-and-breakfast's rowboat, canoe, and bikes are available for guests' use.

The Stout Trout
Bed & Breakfast
W4244 County Highway F
Springbrook, WI 54875
715-466-2790

Apple Crunch Muffins

When the Harlson apples come off the trees in the fall, this recipe comes out of Kathleen Fredricks' recipe files. While these are great muffins her guests enjoy at breakfast, "they are perfect tea muffins, too." Makes 12 muffins.

1 ½ cups flour
½ cup sugar
2 teaspoons baking powder
½ teaspoon salt
½ teaspoon cinnamon
¼ cup butter
1 egg
½ cup milk
1 cup tart apples, unpeeled and shredded

Nut Crunch Topping
¼ cup brown sugar
¼ cup pecans, chopped
½ teaspoon cinnamon

- Preheat oven to 375 degrees.
- In a large bowl, mix together the flour, sugar, baking powder, salt, and cinnamon. Cut in butter, until flour mixture is in the "fine crumb" stage.
- In a separate bowl, combine the egg, milk, and apples. Add to the flour-butter mixture, stirring just to moisten.
- To make the topping, combine the brown sugar, chopped pecans, and cinnamon.
- Spoon into muffin cups, filling ⅔ full. Sprinkle the tops with the nut crunch topping.
- Bake for 20 to 25 minutes, or until golden brown. Serve warm.

Wedgwood Inns

*W*hen Carl Glassman and Dinie Silnutzer-Glassman decided to make career changes, they did their research, worked in the hospitality industry, and then threw caution to the wind. A nineteenth-century home came up for sale, one that Carl had noticed for quite some time, and they started in on the major restoration needed.

The resulting Wedgwood House, named after their collection of china, opened in 1982, just a few blocks from the village center of this historic Bucks County river town. But that was just the beginning — it turned out they enjoyed innkeeping so much, they restored other inns, and now teach classes to aspiring innkeepers, as well.

Their bed-and-breakfasts are nineteenth-century homes on more than two acres of landscaped grounds. Guests can enjoy the gardens, gazebo, and a game of croquet, played in traditional costume, at tea-time in the summer. In the winter, tea and treats are enjoyed fireside in the parlor.

Dinie and Carl offer fresh-baked pastries, warm comforters, a glass of homemade almond liqueur before bed, and other touches to make guests comfortable. They host a number of special events, including historic reenactments, romantic getaways, relaxation retreats and other events created purely for guests' enjoyment.

Wedgwood Inns
111 West Bridge Street
New Hope, PA 18938
215-862-2520
Fax 215-862-2570

Applesauce Raisin Muffins

"The preparations for this recipe actually begin by picking apples at our neighbors' Bucks County orchard. Full of flavor and healthfully low in fat — even lower if nuts are omitted — this recipe smells as good as the muffins taste," said Innkeeper Carl Glassman. Makes 12 muffins.

- ½ cup sugar
- 2 cups flour
- 1½ teaspoons baking powder
- 1 teaspoon baking soda
- ½ teaspoon salt
- 1 teaspoon cinnamon
- ¼ cup pecans, chopped, optional
- 2 egg whites
- 1 tablespoon oil
- 1 cup applesauce
- 1 teaspoon vanilla extract
- ½ cup raisins or currants

- Preheat oven to 350 degrees. Line muffin pan with paper liners or spray with nonstick cooking spray.
- In a large bowl, mix sugar, flour, baking powder, baking soda, salt, cinnamon, and optional pecans.
- Add egg whites, oil, applesauce, vanilla extract, and raisins or currants, beating just to blend in the flour.
- Spoon batter into muffin cups.
- Bake for 25 minutes or until golden brown.

Grandma's House
Bed & Breakfast

*B*uilt in 1860 of bricks made and fired right on the property, Grandma's House, once Innkeeper David Farver's parents' house, rests next to a 16-acre woods; the chestnut woodwork inside the home probably came from the woods. Inside, the home's rooms are quite large, with nine-and-one-half–foot ceilings. In 1987, the Farvers undertook some renovation in preparation for bed-and-breakfast operation. The front porch was rebuilt in the hopes that the innkeepers and their guests would have time to sit and relax there; bathrooms were added or renovated; new windows added; a chestnut ceiling was added in the dining room using wood salvaged from an old shed. The rooms are furnished with many family heirlooms and antiques, handmade quilts, and collections such as rolling pins and old sewing equipment.

Breakfast at Grandma's includes homemade grape juice and grape jelly, made with grapes from the arched grape arbor in the front of the house. Guests are also treated to homemade cinnamon rolls, coffee cakes, muffins, and more, all served at the round oak dining table. The pottery used for serving is specially made for Grandma's House by Marilyn's brother, Gene Tokheim.

Grandma's House Bed & Breakfast
5598 Chippewa Road
Orrville, OH 44667
330-682-5112

Apricot White Chocolate Muffins

"I personally love apricots and chocolate, so this was a natural for me," said Innkeeper Marilyn Farver. "This bakes up into a sweet and flavor-filled muffin." Makes 14 to 15 medium muffins.

    2 cups flour
   ⅓ cup brown sugar
   ⅓ cup sugar
    2 tablespoons baking powder
   ¼ teaspoon salt
    1 cup dried apricots, snipped
   ¾ cup walnuts, chopped
   ¾ cup vanilla chips or white chocolate chunks
   ⅔ cup milk
   ½ cup butter or margarine, melted
    2 eggs, beaten
  1½ teaspoon vanilla extract

- Preheat oven to 350 degrees. Line muffin pan with paper liners or spray with nonstick cooking spray.
- In a medium bowl, combine the flour, brown sugar, sugar, baking powder, salt, snipped apricots, walnuts, and vanilla chips or white chocolate chunks.
- In a separate bowl, mix together the milk, melted butter or margarine, beaten eggs, and vanilla. Add the milk mixture to the flour mixture, stirring until moistened.
- Spoon the batter into muffin cups.
- Bake for 20 to 25 minutes.

Peppertrees Bed & Breakfast Inn

*M*arjorie Martin's yard in Tucson is blessed with two large pepper trees, believed to be as old as her 1905 brick house, and after which her bed-and-breakfast is named. (She also has a lemon tree providing "lemons the size of grapefruit!")

A native of England, Marjorie has decorated her inn with family antiques brought from Britain, and many of her breakfast dishes are old family favorites with an English flavor. She cooks Southwest Tex-Mex cuisine, too, and her creations are so popular she has penned two editions of a Peppertrees cookbook.

Originally, this house had three rooms, a dirt cellar, a back porch for cooking, and an outhouse. It was designed with high ceilings to catch the breezes, and at the time, most Arizonans did their cooking, bathing, and sleeping outside when it was really hot.

Over the years, many additions to the house were made. When Marjorie decided to open it as a B&B, everything was redecorated and a few more additions were made, including a fountain and surrounding patio and garden, where breakfast might be served and where there is always some type of plant in bloom, year-round. Guests at this B&B are only two blocks from the University of Arizona.

Peppertrees Bed & Breakfast Inn
724 East University Boulevard
Tucson, AZ 85719
602-622-7167

Bacon Cheese Muffins

And now for something very different! Leave it to creative Innkeeper Marjorie Martin to provide your breakfast bacon and eggs in a cheesy muffin. Makes 12 muffins.

- 2 cups flour
- ¼ teaspoon salt
- 1 teaspoon baking powder
- 2 tablespoons sugar
- 6 slices bacon, cooked and crumbled
- ½ cup sharp cheese, grated
- 1 egg
- ¼ cup oil
- 1 cup milk

- Preheat oven to 400 degrees. Grease muffin cups.
- Measure the flour, salt, baking powder, sugar, crumbled bacon pieces, and cheese into a large bowl. Stir well, and make a well in the center.
- Beat the egg in a small bowl, and add the oil and milk. Add the egg mixture to the flour mixture, and stir only to moisten.
- Spoon batter into muffin cups.
- Bake for 20 to 25 minutes. Let stand for a few minutes before removing from the pan. Serve warm.

The Graham Bed & Breakfast Inn

*T*he Graham Inn was the first bed-and-breakfast to be built specifically as a B&B in Arizona, and it opened in 1985. An award-winning, South western-style inn, the Graham features a mix of antique, Art Deco, and Southwest furnishings. The six guestrooms have balconies that overlook the stunning red rock region of Sedona. Guests can also enjoy the pool, outdoor spa, bicycles, and sculptures and paintings by local artists.

Seven years after it opened, Carol and Roger Redenbaugh got "red rock fever" and fell in love with Sedona. "We stumbled into the inn and knew it was what we wanted to do," Carol said. They have added their own special touches, from Roger's fresh-roasted coffee and Carol's gourmet breakfasts to an orientation program on the Sedona area.

Four years after entering innkeeping — at a time when many innkeepers are experiencing "burnout" and thinking of selling — Carol and Roger are expanding the Graham Inn. In 1997, four new luxury casitas (individual cottages) opened at the inn. Called Adobe Village, the casitas feature waterfall showers, fireplaces in the bathrooms and more great red rock views. Guests can expect the same personal Redenbaugh touches that makes their stay especially memorable.

The Graham Bed & Breakfast Inn
150 Canyon Circle Drive
Sedona, AZ 86351
Toll-free 800-228-1425
Fax 520-284-0767

Banana Pistachio Muffins

"These muffins are always at hit at the Graham Inn," said Innkeeper Carol Redenbaugh. "We usually serve them with granola pancakes and cinnamon apples." Makes 12 muffins.

1 ½ cups flour
1 ½ teaspoons baking soda
 ¼ teaspoon salt
 ⅛ teaspoon nutmeg
1 ½ cups mashed banana (3 ripe)
 ½ cup sugar
 ⅓ cup brown sugar, packed
 ½ cup butter, melted
 ¼ cup milk
 1 egg
 1 cup shelled pistachio nuts
 1 cup coconut

- Preheat oven to 350 degrees. Grease muffin cups.
- Combine flour, baking soda, salt, and nutmeg in a bowl.
- In a separate bowl, mix together the mashed banana, sugar, brown sugar, butter, milk, and egg. Mix the banana mixture into the flour mixture, and then fold in the nuts.
- Spoon batter into 12 greased muffin cups. Sprinkle with coconut.
- Bake for about 25 minutes. Remove from oven and serve warm with butter.

Angel Arbor
Bed & Breakfast Inn

*V*eteran Houston Innkeeper Marguerite Swanson, with her husband, Dean, opened Angel Arbor Bed-and-Breakfast Inn in September 1995 after a busy six-month restoration. Marguerite successfully operated Durham House B&B Inn, just a half-block away, for ten years before "downsizing" to this slightly-smaller Georgian-style home. Both homes were once owned by Jay L. Durham, a Houston Heights benefactor. As father of seven, he aspired to acquire a house for each of his children, but fell short of that goal because of the Great Depression.

Marguerite, a San Antonio native, easily moved into innkeeping as a profession. "I came from a big family and I was used to entertaining, and I just loved the idea of having people in my house all the time," she said. "I never have a day when I wake up and wish I were doing something else." Durham House quickly established a reputation for gracious accommodations and special occasions, such as unique murder mystery dinners, teas, showers, and small private parties.

In order to have a little more free time, she and Dean bought the elegant red brick residence that is now the Angel Arbor. It has four spacious guestrooms upstairs. The 1923 home, built for Katherine and John McTighe, had most recently been used for offices. The Swansons removed glued-down carpet, refinished the original hardwood floors, installed new bathrooms, and replaced many residential fixtures. They turned the screened porch into a year-round solarium, which overlooks the garden, with Marguerite's favorite angel statue and Dean's favorite vine-covered arbor. Guests are welcome to enjoy the garden, as well as the first-floor parlor, solarium, sunroom, and dining room.

Angel Arbor Bed & Breakfast Inn
848 Heights Boulevard
Houston, TX 77007
713-868-4654
Toll-free 800-722-8788

Banana Walnut Whole-Wheat Muffins

It's not uncommon for Innkeeper Marguerite Swanson to send her business guests off to meetings with a batch of these muffins, "instead of them stopping for donuts or something. These are more healthy, especially for business people about to meet with a health-conscious pharmaceutical company or a nurses group," she noted. That means she at least doubles this batch! Makes 12 muffins.

```
    1   cup whole-wheat flour
    1   cup flour
    1   teaspoon baking soda
    1   teaspoon baking powder
   ¼    teaspoon salt
   ½    cup margarine or butter, softened
   ½    cup sugar
    2   eggs
  1½    cups mashed banana (3 ripe)
   ¼    cup milk
    1   teaspoon vanilla extract
    1   cup walnuts, coarsely chopped
```

- Preheat oven to 375 degrees. Grease muffin cups.
- In a large bowl, stir together the whole-wheat flour, flour, baking soda, baking powder, and salt.
- In a separate bowl, cream the butter and sugar; beat in eggs. Stir in the mashed banana, milk, and vanilla.
- Gently stir the banana mixture into the flour mixture; stir in the walnuts.
- Spoon the batter into prepared muffin cups.
- Bake for 25 minutes or until toothpick inserted in middle comes out clean.

Victorian Treasure
Bed & Breakfast Inn

*K*imberly and Todd Seidl offer guest accommodations in two restored Queen Anne Victorians with extraordinary architectural details and thoughtful contemporary conveniences. The 1897 Bissell Mansion, built by an entrepreneur and state senator, had been a single-family dwelling for sixty years, and it maintains many original fixtures. The 1893 Palmer House, with stained and leaded glass and rich carved woods, also has been restored by the Seidls and now boasts romantic fireplace and whirlpool suites.

Whichever home guests choose, their stay will include a decadent "from scratch" breakfast. Served in the formal dining room of the Bissell Mansion, breakfast is a timeless affair during which guests can easily imagine themselves enjoying breakfast nearly a century ago in the same setting.

The Seidls, educated and experienced in hotel and restaurant management, are an enterprising couple who bought an operating inn, then improved business so much they bought another mansion in town in which to expand. They laughingly describe themselves as "persnickety neatnicks" with high standards who are "genuinely interested in exceeding guests' expectations." With plush robes, canopy beds, down-filled comforters, and other amenities, they most often succeed in doing so. Their sister inns are in the quaint town of Lodi, located in the scenic Lake Wisconsin recreational area, close to Madison, Devil's Lake, Baraboo, and Spring Green's House on the Rock and American Players Theater, with a renown outdoor Shakespearean festival.

Victorian Treasure Bed & Breakfast Inn
115 Prairie Street
Lodi, WI 53555
608-592-5199
Toll-free 800-859-5199

Black Bottom Muffins

Rich and cheesecake-like, these muffins could be served for dessert, tea, or breakfast. Don't overbake them, or the cream cheese topping will be dry. Makes 12 muffins.

¾ cup semi-sweet chocolate, chopped, or chips
⅓ cup butter
1¾ cups flour
1 teaspoon baking soda
½ teaspoon salt
½ cup buttermilk
½ cup sugar
1 egg, lightly beaten
1½ teaspoons vanilla extract

Topping

12 ounces (1½ packages) cream cheese, softened
½ cup sugar
1 tablespoon flour
1 egg, lightly beaten
⅛ teaspoon almond extract
½ cup toasted, slivered almonds, divided

- Preheat oven to 375 degrees. Grease muffin cups (paper liners are not recommended).
- In a glass bowl, melt chocolate and butter by microwaving on high for 20-second intervals, stirring after each interval until melted. Cool. While the mixture is cooling, mix flour, baking soda, and salt in a large bowl. Set aside.
- Meanwhile, make the topping. In a bowl of an electric mixer, beat together the cream cheese, sugar, flour, egg, and almond extract. Stir in ¼ cup of the almonds by hand. Set aside.
- In a small bowl, whisk together the cooled chocolate mixture, buttermilk, sugar, egg, and vanilla.
- In the large bowl with the flour mixture, stir in the chocolate-buttermilk mixture. Spoon chocolate batter evenly into muffin cups. Top with the cream cheese topping batter. Sprinkle the remaining ¼ cup of the almonds on top.
- Bake for 20 to 25 minutes or until a knife inserted into the middle comes out with no chocolate batter; the top of the cheesecake layer may crack slightly, but it should still be white. Serve cooled.

Holden House 1902 Bed & Breakfast Inn

*E*legant breakfasts are the hallmark of Holden House. The dining room fare may include some of the herbs or edible flowers that were snipped fresh that morning from the inn's garden. And hungry guests always appreciate the fresh Walnut and White Chocolate Chocolate Chunk Cookies tempting them from the bottomless cookie jar.

Built by Isabel Holden, this 1902 storybook Victorian, its carriage house, and adjacent 1898 Victorian, reside on a tree-lined street of Victorian-era homes near the "old Colorado City" historic district. Innkeepers Sallie and Welling Clark bought and restored the home in 1985 and filled it with antiques and family heirlooms. Continuing with renovation, the carriage house opened in 1990, and the adjacent Rose Victorian began accommodating guests in 1994. Guestrooms in each are named for mining towns in which the Holdens owned interests. But they are hardly reflective of a hardscrabble life, sporting oversized whirlpool tubs, fireplaces, queen beds, and private sitting areas.

Sallie and Welling and their staff insist on friendly service and seeing to their guests' comfort. They are happy to help plan an itinerary to explore the stunning Pikes Peak Region. Guests can take the cog railway to the top of the 14,110-foot, snow-capped Pikes Peak, meander through the towering red rocks at Garden of the Gods, tour the U.S. Air Force Academy or U.S. Olympic Training Center, shop, visit museums and historic sites, white-water raft, or gamble in historic Cripple Creek.

Holden House

1102 West Pikes Peak Avenue
Colorado Springs, CO 80904
719-471-3980

Blueberry Corn Muffins

"This recipe is calculated for 6,000-foot altitude," notes Innkeeper Sallie Clark, "so a tablespoon or so less flour may be appropriate for lower altitudes." The tartness of the blueberries and buttermilk, the sweetness of the molasses and the texture of the cornmeal make a "wonderful blending of flavors." Makes 12 muffins.

   1 cup yellow cornmeal
   1¼ cups low-fat buttermilk
   1½ cups flour
   1½ teaspoons baking powder
   1½ teaspoons baking soda
   ⅓ cup sugar
   1 egg, slightly beaten, or equivalent egg substitute
   ¼ cup dark molasses
   ⅓ cup butter or margarine, melted
   1 cup fresh or frozen blueberries

- Preheat oven to 400 degrees. Spray muffin cups with nonstick cooking spray.
- Mix together the cornmeal and buttermilk, and set aside for about 20 minutes.
- Mix together the flour, baking powder, baking soda, and sugar. With a wire whip, stir in the egg, molasses, melted butter, and cornmeal-buttermilk mixture until thoroughly moistened. Fold the blueberries into the corn mixture with a spoon.
- Evenly fill the muffin cups.
- Bake for 25 to 30 minutes, or until slightly brown on top. Remove muffins from the oven and allow them to rest a minute or so before removing from the pan.

The Bonnynook Inn

*I*n 1983, Bonnie and Vaughn Franks bought this 1880 mansion, built during the cotton boom, to renovate as a five-guestroom inn. "We soon be came expert caulkers during the six-year renovation," Bonnie notes. The inn opened in 1989, and the Franks soon started serving breakfast favorites such as Applesauce Pancakes, "Pennsylvania Shoofly Squares," and muffins such as these to satisfied guests. Bonnie's mother, whose ancestors provided many of the recipes used at the inn, crocheted the bed spreads and throws, adding to the inn's warmth and cozy atmosphere.

Guests relax in large, antique-filled guestrooms, some with whirlpools, after a day of antique shopping in the historic downtown district, or visiting the many historic sites. Architecture buffs come to Waxahachie to enjoy homes like the Bonnynook Inn, one of the more than 225 properties in Waxahachie listed on the National Register of Historic Places. The Ellis County Courthouse, just two blocks from the inn, is the second most-photographed historic building in the state, complete with gargoyles and other interesting features.

Many of the surrounding Victorian homes can be seen by guests from either the upstairs or downstairs porches. Self-paced walking tours and driving tours are available to Waxahachie's other three national historic districts and to movie locations, where "Tender Mercies" and "Places in the Heart," among others, were filmed.

Bonnie and Vaughn are now involved with the management of a new inn, Etta's Place, in the Sundance Square district of downtown Fort Worth. Located around the corner from the Caravan of Dreams, a jazz nightclub, the inn is to have ten guestrooms, including four suites with kitchens. Guests will enjoy the convenience of being in the 22 square blocks of downtown Forth Worth that makes up the Sundance Square area. The inn is named after the Sundance Kid's schoolteacher girlfriend.

The Bonnynook Inn
414 West Main
Waxahachie, TX 75165
972-938-7207

Brandied Apple Morning Muffins

"I love recipes that keep in the refrigerator for a while. I try to develop as many as I can so that when I have a last-minute guest, there isn't any panic nor dashing off to the store," writes Innkeeper Bonnie Franks. This batter may be held in the refrigerator for three weeks. Double or triple the recipe and bake as needed. Makes 12 large or 18 small muffins.

½ teaspoon baking soda
1 cup buttermilk
1 cup old-fashioned rolled oats
1 apple, peeled and chopped
⅛ cup brandy
½ cup brown sugar
1 egg, beaten
1 cup flour
1 teaspoon salt
1 teaspoon baking powder
1 teaspoon cinnamon
½ teaspoon nutmeg
½ cup margarine, melted and cooled slightly
1 cup golden raisins
½ cup walnuts, finely chopped
½ cup cherry or raspberry preserves

■ Preheat oven to 400 degrees. Grease muffin cups.
■ Completely dissolve baking soda into the buttermilk. Add oats, and stir. Let oats soak in buttermilk mixture for 30 minutes.
■ Place chopped apple into saucepan with brandy. Cook until slightly tender. Cool slightly.
■ Add brown sugar, egg, flour, salt, baking powder, cinnamon, and nutmeg to oat mixture. Add melted margarine, raisins, walnuts, and apple mixture. Mix well by hand.
■ Spoon batter into greased muffin cups, about ⅔ full. Top with 1 teaspoon of preserves.
■ Bake for 25 to 30 minutes or until toothpick inserted in middle comes out clean.

The Doanleigh Inn

*T*he Doanleigh Inn, Kansas City's first bed-and-breakfast, was named after one of the original innkeeper's great-great-great grandmothers, Sarah Doanleigh of Wales. The current innkeepers, Cynthia Brogdon and Terry Maturo, purchased the grand inn in 1985 and have begun extensive renovations of the 1907 Georgian mansion, once a majestic private home.

The couple's interest in innkeeping began after Cynthia spent several years traveling throughout the country on business. Tiring of hotels and seeking more personalized service in a relaxed atmosphere, she began staying in B&Bs and country inns. Today, as innkeepers, Cynthia and Terry try to offer the service and pampering for their business and leisure guests that they would appreciate themselves. Computer modem access in guestrooms, early breakfasts, in-room speaker phones, and other conveniences are all efforts to meet the needs of business travelers. And, while the breakfast may be served as early as 6:00 in the morning., it is still delicious gourmet fare that has earned Cynthia quite a reputation. Guests enjoy evening hors d'oeuvres and wine, as well.

In the heart of Kansas City, the Doanleigh Inn overlooks historic Hyde Park, just 12 minutes from downtown. It is closer still to the famed Country Club Plaza, Hallmark Crown Center, and the University of Missouri, and it is near the Nelson-Atkins Museum of Art and other attractions.

The Doanleigh Inn
217 East 37th Street
Kansas City, MO 64111
816-753-2667
Fax 816-531-5185

Butterscotch Oatmeal Muffins

"Everyone loves these sweet muffins for breakfast," says Innkeeper Cynthia Brogdon, who doubles this recipe. She notes the batter can be kept, covered, in refrigerator for up to seven days. Makes 18 muffins.

1½ cups old-fashioned rolled oats
2 cups buttermilk
1½ cups brown sugar, packed
½ cup butter, melted and cooled
3 eggs
2 cups flour
2 teaspoons baking powder
½ teaspoon salt
¾ teaspoon baking soda
¾ cup butterscotch chips

- Preheat oven to 350 degrees. Grease muffin cups.
- In a large bowl, combine the oats, buttermilk, and brown sugar. Set aside.
- In a separate bowl, combine the butter and eggs. Add to the oats, and mix well.
- Sift together the flour, baking powder, salt, and baking soda. Stir in the butterscotch chips. Add the flour mixture to the oat mixture.
- Spoon the batter into muffin cups.
- Bake for 15 minutes.

The Stout Trout
Bed & Breakfast

*I*nnkeeper Kathleen Fredricks found this former fishing lodge, located on Gull Lake in the Hayward Lakes region, when she returned to her home state after living in California. The building, complete with paint-on-velvet Elvis, needed a year's worth of major work. She gutted it and set to work, keeping only the original plank floors, and creating four large guestrooms.

Guests dine downstairs in the great room overlooking Gull Lake. In the winter, the forty acres behind the bed-and-breakfast are popular with cross-country skiing guests. In the summer, guests can fish for bass out front, or trout fish, canoe or tube the Namekagon River, swim, or berry-pick nearby. The bed-and-breakfast's rowboat, canoe, and bikes are available for guests' use.

The Stout Trout
Bed & Breakfast
W4244 County Highway F
Springbrook, WI 54875
715-466-2790

Caramel Pecan Upside-Down Muffins

"These are the first muffins I made after getting 'the basics' in Home Ec class," recalled Innkeeper Kathleen Fredricks. "Suffice to say, they've been in my repertoire for years!" See for yourself. Makes 12 muffins.

⅓ cup brown sugar
2 tablespoons butter, softened
   pecan halves, 3 to 4 per muffin cup
1 cup flour
1 cup quick-cooking oats
¼ cup sugar
3 teaspoons baking powder
½ teaspoon salt
½ teaspoon baking soda
¼ cup butter
1 egg
1 cup buttermilk

- Preheat oven to 400 degrees.
- Blend brown sugar with the 2 tablespoons butter. Evenly pat brown sugar-butter mixture into the muffin cups. Arrange the pecan halves on top of the mixture.
- In a large bowl, mix the flour, oats, sugar, baking powder, salt, and baking soda. Cut the butter into the mixture.
- Blend the egg with the buttermilk, and stir into the flour mixture until just dampened.
- Spoon batter into muffin cups, on top of pecan halves.
- Bake for 15 to 20 minutes.

Inn at Cedar Crossing

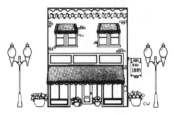

*A*t the Inn at Cedar Crossing, Innkeeper Terry Wulf's guests are treated to a hearty continental breakfast that might include these muffins or a number of other wonderful creations by the Inn's pastry chef, Jeanne Demers. This Historic Register mercantile building was erected in 1884, with shops at street level and merchant's quarters upstairs. In 1985, Terry, a banker who was active in local historic preservation, purchased the building to remake into an inn. After extensive restoration, the upstairs was transformed into an inviting inn, and, later, the street level became an acclaimed restaurant with Victorian era decor.

Today, the inn has nine guestrooms with period antiques, custom-crafted poster and canopied beds, and elegant decor. Many of the guestrooms have fireplaces graced with antique mantels, double whirlpool tubs, private porches, and televisions and VCRs hidden in armoires. All of the rooms feature plump down-filled comforters and decorator fabrics, wallpapers, and linens. The Gathering Room is a relaxing spot for guests to gather by the fireplace and enjoy locally-pressed apple cider, popcorn, and those homemade cookies fresh from the Inn's baking kitchen.

This Inn's restaurant has been named as one of the Top 25 restaurants in the state by the *Milwaukee Journal*. Open daily for all three meals, the restaurant specializes in fresh ingredients, enticingly-prepared entrées, and sinful desserts, and a casual pub serves liquid refreshments. The Inn's guests head out to enjoy Door County's hiking, biking, antiquing, shopping, golfing, or just poking along the back roads of this scenic peninsula bordered by Lake Michigan.

Inn at Cedar Crossing

336 Louisiana Street
Sturgeon Bay, WI 54235
414-743-4200
Fax 414-743-4422

Carrot Bran Muffins

Pastry Chef Jeanne Demers created this wonderful recipe. It's now a favorite among guests, especially in the fall and winter, with its comforting cinnamon aroma. Makes 12 to 13 large muffins.

2	cups wheat bran
4	eggs
1½	cups oil
1½	cups brown sugar
¼	cup molasses
3	cups carrots, grated
1	cup raisins
1	cup nuts, chopped (any type)
3	cups flour
1	teaspoon baking soda
½	tablespoon baking powder
¾	teaspoon salt
1	tablespoon cinnamon

- Preheat oven to 350 degrees. Line muffin pan with paper liners, and spray top of pan with nonstick cooking spray.
- In a large bowl, combine the bran, eggs, oil, brown sugar, molasses, and grated carrot. Add the raisins and nuts.
- In a separate bowl, combine the flour, baking soda, baking powder, salt, and cinnamon. Add the flour mixture to the bran-carrot mixture, stirring by hand until just moistened.
- Fill muffin cups to heaping.
- Bake for 25 minutes until golden brown on top and toothpick inserted in middle comes out clean.

Peppertrees Bed & Breakfast Inn

*M*arjorie Martin's yard in Tucson is blessed with two large pepper trees, believed to be as old as her 1905 brick house, and after which her bed-and-breakfast is named. (She also has a lemon tree providing "lemons the size of grapefruit!")

A native of England, Marjorie has decorated her inn with family antiques brought from Britain, and many of her breakfast dishes are old family favorites with an English flavor. She cooks Southwest Tex-Mex cuisine, too, and her creations are so popular she has penned two editions of a Peppertrees cookbook.

Originally, this house had three rooms, a dirt cellar, a back porch for cooking, and an outhouse. It was designed with high ceilings to catch the breezes, and at the time, most Arizonans did their cooking, bathing, and sleeping outside when it was really hot.

Over the years, many additions to the house were made. When Marjorie decided to open it as a B&B, everything was redecorated and a few more additions were made, including a fountain and surrounding patio and garden, where breakfast might be served and where there is always some type of plant in bloom, year-round. Guests at this B&B are only two blocks from the University of Arizona.

Peppertrees Bed & Breakfast Inn
724 East University Boulevard
Tucson, AZ 85719
602-622-7167

Chili Cheese Corn Muffins

"In the Southwest part of the U.S., we are inspired to use the typical foods of the Indian and Spanish that are our heritage," Innkeeper Marjorie Martin explained. She often cooks and bakes for guests with white, blue, or yellow cornmeal, several kinds of chili peppers, cactus fruit, citrus fruit, cilantro, chocolate, and cinnamon. "These muffins are a collaboration of our favorite corn muffins, cheese, and green chilis." Makes 15 muffins.

   1 cup yellow cornmeal
  ¼ cup sugar
  1 teaspoon salt
  1 cup flour
  1 tablespoon baking powder
  1 cup milk
  ⅓ cup oil
  1 egg
  1 cup medium sharp cheese, grated
  1 4-ounce can green chilis, chopped

- Preheat oven to 400 degrees. Grease muffin cups.
- In a medium bowl, sift cornmeal, sugar, salt, flour, and baking powder together.
- In a separate bowl, blend together the milk, oil, and egg. Mix the milk mixture with the cornmeal mixture. Fold in the grated cheese and the chopped chilis.
- Fill the greased muffin cups ¾ full.
- Bake for about 20 minutes. Let stand for 5 minutes before turning out on a rack to cool. Serve warm.

The Old Iron Inn
Bed & Breakfast

*T*he Old Iron Inn is located in Aroostook County, in northern Maine, far from the touristed areas along the coast. This area is so unusual that it is simply known as "The Country" throughout Maine and much of the rest of New England, explain innkeepers Kate and Kevin McCartney. Visitors will find that "The Country" has the largest geographic area but lowest population density in the Eastern United States, is home to several active Swedish communities, and half the population speaks French. Kate and Kevin opened the inn in 1992, partly because there were few bed-and-breakfast inns in this scenic area and partly because they enjoy meeting a wide variety of travelers. As part of her studies as an undergraduate, Kate spent a semester in England and traveled around Europe, staying at B&Bs. She enjoyed the experience, and has based the Old Iron Inn on the European model, accommodating guests' assorted comfort and dietary needs.

The name of the inn comes from the McCartney's collection of antique irons that decorates the house. They've found irons hold considerable diversity despite their use as an ordinary household appliance. The McCartneys are avid readers and their specialized libraries include mysteries, books about Abraham Lincoln, and aviation history. The reading room, open to guests, also boasts forty magazine subscriptions. A monthly music night is also open to guests. The inn is a turn-of-the-century Arts and Crafts style house, with the original interior oak woodwork intact. The McCartneys have made sensitive renovations, striving to maintain its historical integrity. The four guestrooms are each furnished in oak with highback beds. "There is no television on the premises," said Kate. "There are simply too many other things to do."

The Old Iron Inn Bed & Breakfast
155 High Street
Caribou, ME 04736
207-492-4766

Chocolate Cheesecake Muffins

"These are very special muffins, full of flavor and richness. I usually make these for breakfast if a guest is having a birthday," writes Innkeeper Kate McCartney. "They also make decadent desserts: While hot out of the oven, split open, put a scoop of French vanilla ice cream in the middle, and drizzle with chocolate sauce." Makes 6 large muffins.

> 1 cup flour
> ½ cup sugar
> 2 teaspoons baking powder
> ¼ cup cocoa powder
> ½ cup milk
> 1 egg
> ¼ cup oil
> 1 teaspoon almond extract

Filling

> 4 ounces cream cheese, softened
> ¼ cup powdered sugar
> 2 drops almond extract
> 1 tablespoon cornstarch

- The night before, mix together the flour, sugar, baking powder, and cocoa powder in a large bowl. Cover with a clean dishtowel, and set aside.
- Preheat oven to 350 degrees. Grease muffin cups.
- In a small bowl, make filling: Beat together the cream cheese, powdered sugar, almond extract, and cornstarch until uniformly fluffy. Set aside.
- In a separate bowl, beat together milk, egg, oil, and almond extract. Add milk mixture to flour mixture. Mix just until you no longer see any dry bits in the batter.
- Fill the bottoms of the muffin cups with approximately 2 tablespoons of batter (or about ⅓ full). Dab a spoonful of the cream cheese filling in the middle of each muffin cup, making sure that the filling is not touching any of the sides. Cover up the cream cheese with the rest of the batter, filling muffin cups until they are full. Work as quickly as you can, so the cream cheese doesn't sink to the bottom.
- Bake for 15 to 20 minutes, depending on your oven. "They are done when they smell so good you can't stand it any longer," writes Kate.

Black Dog Inn

*I*n 1910, John Manford sold his hotel in downtown Estes Park to build his home and construct cabins. The home is now the Black Dog Inn (and, unfortunately, the cabins on the land next door are now gone). "The warmth of knotty pine, hardwood floors, and big stone fireplace transport our guests to a time not so long ago, when life was not so hectic," said Pete Princehorn.

Pete and Jane opened this home as a bed-and-breakfast in 1990. It is snuggled in among towering pines and aspen on rolling acreage, with an expansive view of Lumpy Ridge and Estes Valley. Decorated with family antiques, each of the Black Dog Inn's four guestrooms is named for the mountain peaks that surround the inn: Sundance Mountain, Snowdrift Peak, Mummy Mountain, and Mt. Olympus.

Jane and Pete have had experience hiking, skiing, and snowshoeing in Rocky Mountain National Park, and they are happy to share books, maps, and back-country knowledge with their guests. A footpath, running in front of the inn, leads to nearby attractions: cross-country skiing, backpacking, rock climbing, fishing, llama trekking, white-water rafting, and more. The fairgrounds, a public pool, a golf course, and restaurants are all within walking distance.

Black Dog Inn
P.O. Box 4659
Estes Park, CO 80517
970-586-0374

Chocolate Mint Muffins

"For years, our family has been enjoying these yummy chocolate treats," said Innkeeper Jane Princehorn. "At Christmas, they are especially festive when frosted with a powdered sugar frosting and crushed red peppermint candies." She does not adjust the recipe, despite baking at the 7,600-foot elevation in Estes Park. Makes 12 muffins.

1½ cups flour
½ cup sugar
4 tablespoons cocoa powder
1½ teaspoons baking powder
½ teaspoon salt, optional
½ teaspoon baking soda
1 egg
¾ cup milk
¼ oil
¼ teaspoon peppermint extract
12 small, round chocolate mint patties
2 ounces unsweetened chocolate, melted
powdered sugar

- Preheat oven to 375 degrees. Line muffin pan with paper liners or spray with nonstick cooking spray.
- In a large bowl, combine flour, sugar, cocoa powder, baking powder, salt, and baking soda. Stir to blend. Make a well in the center of the dry ingredients.
- In a small bowl, whisk the egg, milk, oil, and peppermint extract. Pour into the well in the dry ingredients. Stir until just mixed; don't overmix.
- Divide ½ of the batter among the 12 muffin cups. Place 1 unwrapped mint patty in the center of each muffin, and cover with the remaining batter.
- Bake for 20 minutes. Sprinkle tops with powdered sugar. Let cool for 5 minutes before serving.

The McCallum House

A low-fat, low-cholesterol breakfast is served family-style in the dining room of Nancy and Roger Danley, who have operated this home as a bed-and-breakfast since 1983, one of the first B&Bs to open in Texas.

The Danleys bought this 1907 home from the heirs of Jane and A. N. McCallum. A. N. was Austin's school superintendent for 39 years. Jane was a suffragist who helped organize the "Petticoat Lobby" for human service reforms in Texas (signs and other memorabilia grace the stairway). She served under two governors as secretary of state. They also raised five children in this large house, which Jane designed while she was pregnant with her fifth child.

Nancy and Roger started innkeeping as an experiment, with just one guestroom in 1983. Today, the Danleys have three guestrooms on the second floor, a garden apartment and a large suite in the dormered third floor called "Jane's Loft," which Roger built.

Their inn is a popular destination for those visiting the University of Texas at Austin, about eight blocks away, or Austin's many attractions. The Danleys love Austin, a wonderful city close to the Texas Hill Country, and they're happy to help guests explore the area.

The McCallum House

613 West 32nd
Austin, TX 78705
512-451-6744
Fax 512-451-4752

Cocoa Banana Muffins

"These are very 'chocolatey' and the bananas give them a nice, rich quality," promises Innkeeper Nancy Danley. Nancy has made low-fat breakfasts a satisfying art form, and these muffins are one example of her cooking in which guests don't miss the calories from fat. Makes 10 to 12 large muffins.

½ cup unsweetened applesauce
¾ cup sugar
1 cup mashed bananas (2 ripe)
¼ cup milk
2 egg whites, lightly beaten
1 teaspoon vanilla extract
1½ cups flour
½ cup "flour combo" (2 parts old-fashioned rolled oats and 1 part wheat bran, ground to a coarse flour in food processor)
⅓ cup cocoa powder
2 teaspoons baking soda
2 teaspoons cinnamon

- Preheat oven to 375 degrees. Grease muffin cups.
- Combine the applesauce, sugar, mashed banana, milk, egg whites, and vanilla well.
- In a separate bowl, sift the flour, flour combo, cocoa powder, baking soda, and cinnamon together. Combine well.
- Add the applesauce mixture to the flour mixture, blending until just mixed.
- Spoon into muffin cups.
- Bake for 20 minutes, being careful not to overbake.

The Buttonwood Inn

*O*riginally constructed as a four-room Cape Cod–style farm house in 1820, the Buttonwood Inn is today a nine-guestroom bed-and-breakfast. Innkeepers Peter and Claudia Needham bought the inn after a "write an essay, win an inn" contest sparked their imaginations. Ten months and thirty properties later, the Buttonwood opened its doors. Each morning a full breakfast is provided, featuring award-winning muffins and special entrées. A special treat for guests, candlelit dinners are served on Saturdays during January and February.

The Buttonwood Inn's abundant common space gives guests plenty of room to move around in, and makes it an ideal gathering place for groups of nine to twenty. From the formal dining room to the lower-level common room, the inn has a comfortable feel.

Although the inn is situated on a quiet, secluded road, North Conway's shops, restaurants, and other attractions remain convenient. In the summer, guests can stroll the inn's five acres of lawns and award-winning gardens, and enjoy the large in-ground swimming pool, Adirondack chairs, badminton, and horseshoes. Hiking trails go right off the back of the property. In the winter, those same hiking trails connect to 65 kilometers of groomed cross-country ski trails, part of a system of ski trails in the Mt. Washington Valley area that make up the country's largest network. Other wintertime attractions include downhill skiing, snowshoeing, ice climbing, skating, and sleigh riding.

The Buttonwood Inn

P.O. Box 1817
Mt. Surprise Road
North Conway, NH 03860
603-356-2625
Fax 603-356-3140

Coconut Muffins

These are Innkeeper Claudia Needham's absolute favorite muffins, and she gets co-inn-keeper/spouse/baker Peter Needham to make them as often as possible. Unfortunately, there are rarely leftovers for the innkeepers to enjoy! Makes 12 muffins.

       2 cups flour
       1 cup sugar
    2½ teaspoons baking powder
       ½ teaspoon salt
       8 tablespoons margarine, melted and cooled
       2 eggs, lightly beaten
       8 ounces plain yogurt
       ½ teaspoon coconut extract
       3 ounces sweetened grated coconut
       ½ cup chocolate chips, optional

- Preheat oven to 375 degrees. Grease muffin cups.
- In a large bowl, mix the flour, sugar, baking powder, and salt. Set aside.
- In a separate bowl, mix the melted margarine, eggs, yogurt, coconut extract, and grated coconut.
- Add the margarine mixture to the flour mixture. Stir in the chocolate chips.
- Spoon into muffin cups.
- Bake for about 18 minutes or until done.

Just-N-Trails Country Inn

A third-generation dairy farm, the Just-N-Trails Country Inn property has been in the Justin family since 1914. In 1985, Don and Donna Justin opened ten kilometers of cross-country ski trails, and the B&B opened a year later. The award-winning Just-N-Trails is set among the scenic wooded hills and valleys of southwestern Wisconsin, near Sparta. The cozy 1920s farmhouse with four guestrooms is complemented by three private luxury cottages: the Granary, the Little House on the Prairie, and the Paul Bunyan — the last two are log cabins.

Donna treats her guests, hungry from the previous day's worth outdoor activities, to a four-course breakfast that features homemade muffins, granola, yogurt, applesauce or fresh fruit, an entrée, and of course coffee, tea, and juice. Area attractions include $12\frac{1}{2}$ kilometers of private, groomed cross-country ski trails, snowtubing, snowshoeing, hiking, biking on the Elroy-Sparta Trail, canoeing, and visiting the nearby Amish community, state and national parks and forests, and quaint antique shops. Guests are encouraged to play with the rabbits, kittens, Peter the pygmy goat, and chickens on this working farm. Donna also notes that they serve dinner on Friday and Saturday nights, and they can accommodate meetings, parties, and reunions for up to 35 people.

Just-N-Trails Country Inn

7452 Kathryn Avenue
Sparta, WI 54656
608-269-4522
Fax 608-269-3280

Craisin Chocolate Chip Muffins

For those with food allergies, Innkeeper Donna Justin notes that there are no eggs or oil in this recipe. Oat bran flour or rice flour adds an interesting texture and is more health-ful, and oat bran and rice flour can be eaten by people who are allergic to wheat flour. "My guests with allergies love that, because they can eat what everyone else is eating and not feel neglected," writes Donna. White flour can be used, but decrease the baking powder to one teaspoon. Makes 12 muffins.

    ¾ cup sugar
    8 ounces low-fat ricotta cheese
    2 cups oat bran or rice flour
    1 teaspoon baking soda
 1½ teaspoons baking powder
   ½ teaspoon salt
    1 teaspoon orange rind, grated
    1 cup orange juice
    1 cup craisins (dried cranberries)
   ½ cup chocolate chips
   ½ cup pecans, chopped

Topping

   ¼ cup sugar
    1 teaspoon cinnamon

- Preheat oven to 375 degrees. Line muffin pan with paper liners or spray with nonstick cooking spray.
- In a mixing bowl, beat sugar and ricotta cheese.
- In a separate bowl, sift oat bran or rice flour, baking soda, baking powder, salt, and grated orange rind together. Alternately add the flour mixture and the orange juice to the sugar and cheese.
- Fold in the craisins, chocolate chips, and chopped pecans.
- Using an ice cream scoop, spoon the batter into muffin cups.
- Make a topping by mixing the sugar and cinnamon. Sprinkle the topping on top of the muffin batter.
- Bake for 20 minutes or until golden brown.

Fairlea Farm Bed & Breakfast

*G*uests at Fairlea Farm Bed & Breakfast enjoy a spectacular view of vast pastures and the Blue Ridge Mountains. "On a clear day, if you know exactly where to look, you can even see cars in the distance along Skyline Drive in Shenandoah National Park," said Innkeeper Susan Longyear.

Fairlea Farm is a working sheep and cattle farm within two blocks of the center of the historic village of Little Washington, Virginia. George Washington surveyed and laid out plans for the village when he was 17-years-old, note the Longyears. Susan and Walt opened the fieldstone manor house as a four-guestroom inn in order to share the peacefulness of the farm life with travelers.

In addition to Shenandoah National Park, plenty of attractions and activities can keep guests as busy as they like to be. Nearby are craft and antique shops, art galleries, vineyards and wineries, and Civil War battlefields. Those who love outdoor activities can visit Luray Caverns, hike, ride horses, golf, and fish close by.

Fairlea Farm Bed & Breakfast
P.O. Box 124
636 Mt. Salem Avenue
Washington, VA 22747
540-675-3679
Fax 540-675-1064

Cranberry Cream Cheese Muffins

"I make sure that I stock our freezer full of cranberries every year so I can serve these delicious muffins year-round," said Innkeeper Susan Longyear. "They taste so great that our guests never leave any leftovers in the serving basket at the end of breakfast." Makes 24 muffins.

   1 **cup butter, softened**
   1 **8-ounce package cream cheese, softened**
1½ **cups sugar**
1½ **teaspoons vanilla extract**
   4 **eggs**
   2 **cups flour**
1½ **teaspoon baking powder**
  ½ **teaspoon salt**
   2 **cups fresh or frozen cranberries (or blueberries or raspberries), dusted with 2 tablespoons flour**
  ½ **cup pecans or walnuts, chopped**

- Preheat oven to 350 degrees. Line muffin pan with paper liners or spray with nonstick cooking spray.
- In a mixing bowl, beat together the butter, cream cheese, sugar, and vanilla extract. Add the eggs, 1 at a time, beating well after each.
- In a separate bowl, combine the flour, baking powder, and salt. Add to the butter mixture gradually. Fold in cranberries and nuts.
- Spoon batter into greased muffin cups.
- Bake for 25 to 30 minutes, or until golden and toothpick inserted in middle comes out clean. Let muffins stand on a cooling rack for about 3 minutes before removing from the pans.

Old Thyme Inn

*J*ust thirty minutes south of San Francisco is the Old Thyme Inn, a Queen Anne Victorian built in 1899 by the town's first school principal, now offering seven guestrooms. The bed-and-breakfast rests in the tranquil setting of an English herb garden with more than fifty varieties of herbs and flowers cared for by Innkeepers George and Marcia Dempsey, who bought the B&B in 1991 after retiring from careers as an attorney-turned-banker (for George) and in advertising (for Marcia). Half Moon Bay is a coastal village along the Pacific – within a short walking distance are beaches, shops, art galleries, and restaurants. Whale-watching, golf, horseback riding, tennis, hiking, and biking are just some of the area's activities.

The inn's sumptuous breakfast includes homemade banana bread, quiche, scones, Swedish egg cake with fresh fruit, muffins, frittata, croissants with cheeses and turkey, fresh juice, and coffee and tea.

Old Thyme Inn
779 Main Street
Half Moon Bay, CA 94019
415-726-1616
Fax 415-726-6394

Cranberry Orange Muffins

A variety of homebaked pastries are included in the breakfast at the Old Thyme Inn, and this muffin is always one of the first to disappear, reports George Dempsey, innkeeper. Makes 12 muffins.

2 ½ cups flour
¾ cup sugar
2 teaspoons baking powder
1 teaspoon baking soda
½ teaspoon salt
½ teaspoon ground nutmeg
grated zest of 1 orange
1 cup fresh or frozen cranberries, chopped
½ cup sliced almonds
1 cup buttermilk
1 teaspoon vanilla extract
1 egg
½ cup oil

Topping
3 tablespoons sugar
1 teaspoon cinnamon

- Preheat oven to 400 degrees. Line muffin pan with paper liners or spray with nonstick cooking spray.
- In a large bowl, mix together the flour, sugar, baking powder, baking soda, salt, and nutmeg. Add the orange zest, cranberries, and almonds.
- In another bowl, combine the buttermilk, vanilla, egg, and oil. Add the buttermilk mixture to the flour mixture. Combine with as few strokes as possible.
- Spoon the batter into the prepared muffin cups, filling each ½ to ⅔ full.
- Make a topping by mixing together the 3 tablespoons of sugar with the 1 teaspoon of cinnamon. Sprinkle the batter with the topping.
- Bake for approximately 20 minutes, until the tops are golden and crunchy.

Daly Inn

*C*ornelius Daly built this Colonial Revival home in 1905 for his wife, Annie, and their five children. Cornelius came to the area from Ireland, intent on making his fortune. He and his brothers founded Daly Brothers Mercantile in 1895. The store, which grew to a chain of seven, remained a family-run business for one hundred years. The home is a magnificent example of turn-of-the-century elegance, complete with a third-floor "Christmas ballroom."

The Daly home has been restored to its original elegance, with modern conveniences tastefully added. Each room is furnished with antiques, reflecting the charm of the early 1900s. Guests may enjoy a leisurely morning meal in the sunlit breakfast parlor, on the garden patio, or in the formal dining room, seated before a crackling fire. Wine and hors d'oeuvres are served each evening.

The Inn is located a few blocks from Eureka's Old Town, with shops and restaurants, and beautiful Humboldt Bay. The magnificent Redwoods surround the area, with Redwood National Park to the north and Humboldt Redwood State Park to the south. Hiking, birding, cycling, whale watching, kayaking, antique shopping, and touring galleries of local artists are some of the activities available to guests.

Daly Inn
1125 "H" Street
Eureka, CA 95501
707-445-3638
Fax 707-444-3636

Cran-Blackberry Muffins

"This basic muffin recipe was sent to me by a friend when I first opened my B&B nearly seven years ago," said Sue Clinesmith. "I adapted the recipe for use with blackberries, which are so plentiful in this area. The muffins are quick, not too sweet and leftovers — if any — freeze very well." Makes 12 muffins.

¾ cup milk
½ cup oil
⅓ cup sugar
1 egg
3 teaspoons baking powder
1 teaspoon salt
2 cups flour
1 tablespoon lemon rind, grated
½ cup fresh or frozen cranberries, chopped
¾ cup fresh or frozen blackberries
½ cup hazelnuts, chopped

- Preheat oven to 400 degrees. Spray muffin pan with nonstick cooking spray (or use nonstick muffin pan).
- In a large bowl, combine the milk, oil, sugar, egg, baking powder, salt, flour, and lemon rind.
- Gently fold in the cranberries, blackberries, and nuts.
- Spoon the batter into muffin cups.
- Bake about 20 minutes.

Hoyt House Bed & Breakfast

*B*uilt in about 1905 for the head of a mercantile store, bank president, and political leader, Hoyt House is an outstanding example of Victorian architecture in the Queen Anne style on Florida's picturesque Amelia Island.

Innkeepers Rita and John Kovacevich bought the house in 1993 and converted it into an inn. Antique furnishings, current reproductions, collectibles, and romantic guest chambers — some with fireplaces — combine to encompass Hoyt House guests in warmth. Breakfast fare includes juice, fresh fruit, coffee, a variety of teas, a selection of homemade baked specialties including breads, biscuits, scones, muffins, and a gourmet entrée. The inn offers golf weekends and special themes, such as the Valentine Weekend and Dinner, featuring a gourmet dinner, wine, champagne, and flowers.

Hoyt House is located in the downtown Historic District, which is adorned with impressive architecture, beautiful churches, unique shops, fine antique emporiums, the museum of history, and many fine restaurants. Guests can enjoy magnificent beaches, tennis, sport-fishing, an offshore casino, horseback riding, and historic Fort Clinch.

Hoyt House Bed & Breakfast
804 Atlantic Avenue
Fernandina Beach, FL 32034
904-277-4300
Toll-free 800-432-2085

Cream Cheese Breakfast Cakes

"These sugar-and-spice cakes are great for a morning treat or use as a special part of a brunch," said Innkeeper Rita Kovacevich. She notes that, if preparation time is short, the batch may be made ahead of time and frozen. Makes 12 medium or 24 mini-muffins.

1 ½ cups sugar, divided
2 teaspoons cinnamon
1 ½ cups flour
1 ½ teaspoons baking powder
½ teaspoon salt
¼ teaspoon nutmeg
⅓ cup butter or margarine
1 egg
½ cup milk (skim milk can be used)
3 ounces cream cheese, cubed into 12 or 24 pieces
½ cup butter, melted

- Preheat oven to 350 degrees. Lightly grease muffin pan.
- Combine 1 cup sugar and cinnamon. Set aside.
- In a small bowl, combine flour, baking powder, salt, and nutmeg.
- In another bowl, beat together butter, remaining ½ cup sugar, and the egg. Add flour mixture alternately with milk. Stir until combined.
- Use ½ the batter, filling each cup ⅓ full. Top each with a cube of cream cheese. Top each cup with remaining batter.
- Bake for 20 minutes or until golden on top. Remove from pan immediately.
- Roll in melted butter, then sugar-cinnamon mix. Cover entire muffin.

The Delforge Place

This Texas Hill Country inn is home to many family heirlooms, such as the seven-foot mural map that belonged to Betsy Delforge's great-grandfather, who traveled with Admiral Perry in the 1800s. The inn itself is a carefully restored antique. The dining room was built in 1898 as a one-room "Sunday house," commonly built by farmers who needed accommodations while in town to attend church services or do business. German pioneer Ferdinand Koeppen built this one on a tract of land set aside by the German Emigration Company for a communal garden. It was moved to its present site on Ettie Street, seven blocks from Main Street, and restored in 1975.

Betsy and husband George settled here after George retired from a long career as an aeronautical engineer and Betsy as a dress designer and food consultant for major food companies. Their son, Peter, has also joined the business. The Delforge Place is known in Fredericksburg and beyond for its world-class breakfasts, and offers four antique-filled guestrooms.

The Delforge Place
710 Ettie Street
Fredericksburg, TX 78624
512-997-6212

Date Nut Muffins

"You can omit the salt from this recipe, but make sure to add a dash of lemon extract,"
suggests Betsy Delforge. She adds that this is a great low-fat recipe with a little sweet-
ness to start your day. Makes 12 muffins.

⅔ cup dates, chopped
½ cup boiling water
¼ cup butter or margarine
½ cup sugar
1 egg, or equivalent egg substitute, room temperature
1 cup flour
½ teaspoon baking soda
¼ teaspoon salt
½ cup pecans, chopped
powdered sugar for garnish, optional

■ Preheat oven to 350 degrees. Line muffin pan with paper liners or spray with
nonstick cooking spray
■ In a small bowl, combine the dates with the boiling water; cool to room temperature.
■ In a mixing bowl, cream the butter or margarine with the sugar and egg until
light and fluffy.
■ In a separate bowl, stir together the flour, baking soda, and salt; add to the
creamed butter mixture alternately with the date mixture just to combine. Stir
in the chopped nuts.
■ Fill muffin pans ½ full.
■ Bake for 14 to 18 minutes. Sprinkle cooled muffins with powdered sugar, if
desired.

Inn at Cedar Crossing

*A*t the Inn at Cedar Crossing, Innkeeper Terry Wulf's guests are treated to a hearty continental breakfast that might include these muffins or a number of other wonderful creations by the Inn's pastry chef, Jeanne Demers. This Historic Register mercantile building was erected in 1884, with shops at street level and merchant's quarters upstairs. In 1985, Terry, a banker who was active in local historic preservation, purchased the building to remake into an inn. After extensive restoration, the upstairs was transformed into an inviting inn, and, later, the street level became an acclaimed restaurant with Victorian era decor.

Today, the inn has nine guestrooms with period antiques, custom-crafted poster and canopied beds, and elegant decor. Many of the guestrooms have fireplaces graced with antique mantels, double whirlpool tubs, private porches, and televisions and VCRs hidden in armoires. All of the rooms feature plump down-filled comforters and decorator fabrics, wallpapers, and linens. The Gathering Room is a relaxing spot for guests to gather by the fireplace and enjoy locally-pressed apple cider, popcorn, and those homemade cookies fresh from the Inn's baking kitchen.

This Inn's restaurant has been named as one of the top 25 restaurants in the state by the *Milwaukee Journal*. Open daily for all three meals, the restaurant specializes in fresh ingredients, enticingly-prepared entrées, and sinful desserts, and a casual pub serves liquid refreshments. The Inn's guests head out to enjoy Door County's hiking, biking, antiquing, shopping, golfing, or just poking along the back roads of this scenic peninsula bordered by Lake Michigan.

Inn at Cedar Crossing
336 Louisiana Street
Sturgeon Bay, WI 54235
414-743-4200
Fax 414-743-4422

Door County Cherry Almond Muffins

Travelers often come to Door County for a taste of its famous cherry crop. At this inn, guests easily get their fill. The tart red cherries might be found not only in these popular muffins, but also as a glaze for chicken, in a sweet dessert torte, and in jars of jam and chutney waiting to be enjoyed at home. Makes 13 large muffins.

- 4 cups flour
- 1 cup sugar
- 1 ½ teaspoons salt
- 1 ½ tablespoons baking powder
- ½ cup butter
- 2 cups tart cherries, drained
- 1 cup sliced almonds
- 2 eggs
- 1 ½ cups milk, approximately
- ¾ teaspoon almond extract

- Preheat oven to 350 degrees. Line muffin pan with paper liners, and spray top of pan with nonstick cooking spray.
- In a bowl, combine the flour, sugar, salt, and baking powder. Cut in the butter until mixture looks like coarse cornmeal. By hand, stir in the cherries and almonds.
- Break eggs into a 2-cup measure, and add enough milk, approximately 1 ½ cups, to equal 2 cups. Add the almond extract. Stir the milk mixture into the flour mixture by hand, until just moistened.
- Fill the muffin cups to heaping.
- Bake for 25 minutes, or until golden brown and toothpick inserted in middle comes out clean.

Rancho San Gregorio

A hearty breakfast at the Rancho San Gregorio always features produce organically grown on some of the 15 acres surrounding the inn. The morning feast may feature home-baked breads and muffins, artichoke frittata, apple cinnamon crepes, Rancho Soufflé, or Swedish egg cake with wild blackberry sauce. Innkeepers Lee and Bud Raynor invite their guests to hike in the orchard, wade in the creek, play badminton or volleyball, or explore the land, originally part of an 1839 Spanish Land Grant. Nearby are the sandy beaches of Half Moon Bay, redwood groves, recreational trails, and bird and elephant seal sanctuaries.

Just five miles from the Pacific Ocean, the Rancho San Gregorio is an early California Mission-style Inn, with four guestrooms, antique furnishings, Indian rugs and pottery, ranch memorabilia, and private gardens with a gazebo.

Rancho San Gregorio

Route 1, Box 54
5086 La Honda Road
San Gregorio, CA 94074
415-747-0810
Fax 415-747-0184

Double Chocolate Muffins

With no dairy products and no eggs, these muffins (featured on the book's cover) are just the ticket for diet-conscious guests at Rancho San Gregorio. For larger muffins, divide batter among 10 cups instead of 12. Makes 12 muffins.

½ cup orange juice
⅓ cup water
3 tablespoons oil
1 tablespoon vinegar
1 teaspoon vanilla extract
1½ cups flour
½ cup sugar
¼ cup cocoa
1 teaspoon baking soda
¼ teaspoon salt
⅓ cup miniature semisweet chocolate chips
powdered sugar

- Preheat oven to 375 degrees. Line muffin pan with paper liners.
- In a large bowl, whisk together the orange juice, water, oil, vinegar, and vanilla.
- In a separate bowl, mix the flour, sugar, cocoa, baking soda, and salt.
- Stir the flour mixture into the juice mixture, just until all ingredients are moist. Fold in the chips.
- Fill muffin cups ¾ full.
- Bake for 12 minutes, or until a toothpick inserted in the middle comes out clean.
- Remove muffin tray and cool on a rack for several minutes. Sprinkle the tops with powdered sugar before serving the muffins warm.

The Inn at Shallow Creek Farm

*T*he Inn at Shallow Creek Farm is located on a working farm near Orland, California, in the northern Sacramento Valley, an area rich in agriculture and old family traditions. Fresh fruit and local produce are available throughout the area — either direct from the growers or from farmers' markets. In fact, the Inn at Shallow Creek Farm property has orange orchards and grows apples, apricots, peaches, pears, plums, nectarines, pomegranates, persimmons, grapefruit, and more.

Three rooms in the turn-of-the-century country farmhouse and a cottage are furnished with antiques, many of which are family heirlooms. Breakfasts feature fresh fruit and juice from the orchards all year long.

Innkeepers Mary and Kurt Glaeseman have been traveling the B&B route in Europe and the U.S. since the early 1970s. They enjoyed this mode of travel and decided to find a suitable property to start their own B&B, modeled after things they enjoyed at other inns. "The dreams and plans did not include an orchard and farm, but the Shallow Creek Farm property seemed ideal," Mary said. Since 1987, the Glaesemans have welcomed both inn guests and fresh fruit buyers to Shallow Creek Farm.

The Inn at Shallow Creek Farm
4712 Road DD
Orland, CA 95963
916-865-4093

Elderberry Muffins

Innkeeper Mary Glaeseman suggests, "Gather the wild elderberries when they are ripe in late summer. To freeze them, spread the berries on a large pan and put them in the freezer until they are frozen. Then, put them in a freezer bag or a container to measure out later." Makes 15 muffins.

 2 cups flour
½ cup sugar
 1 tablespoon baking powder
¼ teaspoon salt
½ teaspoon allspice
¼ teaspoon nutmeg
½ cup frozen elderberries (a heaping ½ cup)
¼ cup sugar
 2 eggs
½ cup milk
½ cup butter, melted

- Preheat oven to 400 degrees. Line muffin pan with paper liners, and spray top of pan with nonstick cooking spray.
- Sift together in a large bowl the flour, ½ cup of sugar, baking powder, salt, allspice, and nutmeg.
- Mix the frozen elderberries with the ¼ cup of sugar, and let stand briefly.
- In another bowl, beat the eggs. Add the milk and melted butter. Add the egg mixture to the flour mixture, stirring just to moisten. Carefully fold in the sugared elderberries.
- Bake for 20 minutes.

Salisbury House

*W*ashington apples are just one of the fresh fruits that end up as breakfast fare at the Salisbury House. Innkeeper Cathryn Wiese and her mother, Mary, often pick berries at the region's berry farms or enjoy pears and apples from their own trees, and the fruit may end up in muffins, preserves, or on a fruit plate.

Breakfast is served in the dining room of this large, airy home. Downstairs, the home has refinished maple floors and beam ceilings. Upstairs are four guestrooms, all uniquely decorated, and a sun porch. Guests are welcome to play chess in the library, rock on the wrap-around porch, or enjoy the fireplace in the living room.

Mary, who was raised in Seattle, and Cathryn, who has been in Seattle for the past 15 years, opened their bed-and-breakfast in 1984, after living in San Diego for 18 years. Salisbury House is in the beautiful Capitol Hill neighborhood, walking distance to art museums, Volunteer Park, and shops and restaurants. Guests often leave their cars and hop a bus a block away to get to the University of Washington or to explore downtown Seattle's Pike Place Market, piers and Aquarium, historic district, and other attractions.

Salisbury House

750 16th Avenue E
Seattle, WA 98112
206-328-8682
Fax 206-720-1019

Ginger Pear Muffins

If you think the aroma of baking cinnamon and apples is tempting, you haven't discovered ginger and pears. "This recipe started as a cinnamon-apple muffin recipe," said Innkeeper Cathryn Wiese, "but we have a wonderful pear tree at Salisbury House, so I changed the fruit to pears and thought ginger a better companion for them. The molasses was an inspired addition, and the yogurt keeps the muffins moist." Makes 12 to 18 muffins.

  2 cups flour
½ cup brown sugar, packed
  1 teaspoon baking soda
½ teaspoon salt
  2 teaspoons ground ginger
⅛ teaspoon cloves
⅛ teaspoon nutmeg
  1 cup plain yogurt
½ cup oil
  3 tablespoons molasses
  1 egg, beaten
1½ cups fresh pears, unpeeled and diced
½ cup raisins
½ cup nuts, chopped

- Preheat oven to 400 degrees. Line muffin pan with paper liners or spray with nonstick cooking spray.
- Mix flour, brown sugar, baking soda, salt, ginger, cloves, and nutmeg together in a large bowl.
- In a separate bowl, mix the yogurt, oil, molasses, and egg.
- Fold the yogurt mixture into the flour mixture, mixing just until the dry ingredients are moistened.
- Stir in the pears, raisins, and nuts.
- Spoon the batter into muffin cups ⅔ full.
- Bake for 20 minutes.

The Woods House
Bed & Breakfast

*I*n the spring of 1991, Françoise and Lester Roddy moved from Berkeley, California, and purchased the Woods House Bed-and-Breakfast Inn, which has been in existence since 1984. Françoise previously worked in human resources and event planning, and brought calligraphy, cooking, needlecraft, and gardening skills to the innkeeping business; Lester brought over 25 years of business management. Both innkeepers enjoy creating taste treats for their guests, such as fresh peach pie. The Roddys also enjoy setting up theme weekends. The inn hosts popular "murder mystery weekends" at Valentine's Day, Halloween, and New Year's Eve; and in the spring and fall, they host workshops for aspiring innkeepers.

The Woods' half acre of terraced English gardens is shaded by majestic trees and abounds with flowers and herbs and quiet places for guests to relax. The 1908 Craftsman-style inn has six guestrooms, and is just four and one-half blocks from the downtown plaza.

The Woods House Bed & Breakfast

333 North Main Street
Ashland, OR 97520
541-488-1598
Fax 541-482-8027

Ginger Rhubarb Muffins

This recipe is much more than another way to use up the bounty of fresh rhubarb. "This unique flavor combination has a heavenly aroma and looks yummy, too," notes Innkeeper Françoise Roddy. Makes 12 muffins.

- 1¼ cups unbleached flour
- 1 cup whole-wheat flour
- 2 teaspoons baking soda
- 1 teaspoon baking powder
- ½ teaspoon salt
- ¼ cup fresh ginger, grated
- ¾ cup sugar
- 1 cup yogurt
- ½ cup buttermilk
- ⅓ cup oil
- 1 egg
- 1½ cups fresh rhubarb, diced

- Preheat oven to 400 degrees. Line muffin pan with paper liners.
- In a large bowl, mix together the unbleached flour, whole-wheat flour, baking soda, baking powder, salt, and grated ginger.
- In a separate bowl, whisk together the sugar, yogurt, buttermilk, oil, and egg. Stir in the rhubarb, and then the flour mixture. Be careful not to overmix, which makes the muffins tough.
- Fill the muffin cups ¾ full.
- Bake approximately 15 minutes, or until toothpick inserted in middle comes out clean.

Wedgwood Inns

*W*hen Carl Glassman and Dinie Silnutzer-Glassman decided to make career changes, they did their research, worked in the hospitality industry, and then threw caution to the wind. A nineteenth-century home came up for sale, one that Carl had noticed for quite some time, and they started in on the major restoration needed.

The resulting Wedgwood House, named after their collection of china, opened in 1982, just a few blocks from the village center of this historic Bucks County river town. But that was just the beginning — it turned out they enjoyed innkeeping so much, they restored other inns, and now teach classes to aspiring innkeepers, as well.

Their bed-and-breakfasts are nineteenth-century homes on more than two acres of landscaped grounds. Guests can enjoy the gardens, gazebo, and a game of croquet, played in traditional costume, at tea-time in the summer. In the winter, tea and treats are enjoyed fireside in the parlor.

Dinie and Carl offer fresh-baked pastries, warm comforters, a glass of homemade almond liqueur before bed, and other touches to make guests comfortable. They host a number of special events, including historic reenactments, romantic getaways, relaxation retreats and other events created purely for guests' enjoyment.

Wedgwood Inns
111 West Bridge Street
New Hope, PA 18938
215-862-2520
Fax 215-862-2570

Glazed Lemon Blueberry Yogurt Muffins

"Great-tasting, satisfying, and guilt-free, too!" notes Innkeeper Carl Glassman. The Wedgwood innkeepers have adapted this old favorite recipe for today's health-conscious traveler, he notes, "without compromising the taste or texture." Makes 12 large muffins.

2 cups flour
1½ teaspoons baking powder
1 teaspoon baking soda
½ teaspoon salt
½ cup sugar
1 cup low-fat or nonfat yogurt
1 egg, or 2 egg whites
1 teaspoon lemon extract
grated rind of 1 lemon
1 tablespoon oil
2 cups blueberries, washed and sorted

Glaze

juice of 1 lemon
⅓ cup sugar

- Preheat oven to 350 degrees. Line muffin pan with paper liners or spray with nonstick cooking spray.
- Mix together the flour, baking powder, baking soda, salt, and sugar in a large bowl.
- In a separate bowl, combine the yogurt, egg or egg whites, lemon extract, lemon rind, and oil. Mix in the flour mixture, blending just to incorporate the flour.
- Gently fold in the blueberries.
- Scoop batter into cups.
- Bake for 25 minutes or until golden.
- To make the glaze, mix the lemon juice with the ⅓ cup of sugar. Spoon over hot muffin tops, or cool the muffins to touch, and dip the tops into the glaze.

The Adams Hilborne

*W*hen Wendy and David Adams' five children were off to college, making "major life decisions," Wendy and David sat back and decided they were at the age, once again, to make some major decisions, too. Wendy, who trained at the Culinary Institute of America and had a decorating degree, and David, who had a career in finance, looked around for something they could work on together. They hit on innkeeping, and in 1990, they found a bed-and-breakfast in the historic community of Monteagle.

Strong preservationists, they returned the inn to its 14-room, full-service inn origins, and the Adams Edgeworth was soon so successful that they wanted to expand. But they were limited by the size of the historic building, so they purchased a beautiful private home in Chattanooga's historic Fortwood neighborhood. "It was not for sale, so we had to talk the gentleman into selling it to us, and that took six months, and then restoring and redecorating took another six months," Wendy said. But the Adams Hilborne was well worth the time and effort. Built as Chattanooga's mayor's mansion in 1889, it is a magnificent mountain stone building, with its original cherry paneling and curved staircase, hand-carved moldings, and Tiffany glass windows. "There are 16-foot ceilings on the first floor, 14-foot ceilings on the second floor, and 12-foot ceilings on the third floor, so the grandeur of the building has really been maintained," Wendy noted. Listed on the National Register of Historic Places, the inn features a variety of guestrooms, from the Cherry Room with its century-old cherry paneling and wainscoting, to the Lookout Suite with its view of Lookout Mountain. The parlors are filled with antiques and "guests feel like they are still using a grand old private home," Wendy said. The Adams Hilborne is also home to the Repertoire Restaurant and the casual Porch Cafe, an outdoor bistro overlooking the neighborhood.

The Adams Hilborne

801 Vine Street
Chattanooga, TN 37403
615-265-5000
Fax 615-265-5555

Glazed Raspberry Lime Muffins

"What we love about these moist muffins is the waves of flavors that occur when you enjoy them," said Chef Bob Durham. Makes 12 muffins.

- 1½ cups flour
- ¼ cup sugar
- ¼ cup brown sugar, packed
- 2 teaspoons baking powder
- ¼ teaspoon salt
- 1 teaspoon cinnamon
- 1 egg
- ½ cup butter, melted
- ½ cup milk
- 1½ cups fresh raspberries

Topping

- 1 teaspoon dark rum
- 3 teaspoons fresh lime juice
- 1 tablespoon powdered sugar
- ½ cup walnuts, chopped
- ½ cup dark brown sugar
- 1 teaspoon cinnamon
- ¼ cup flour
- 2 tablespoons butter, melted

- Preheat oven to 350 degrees. Line muffin pan with paper liners.
- Combine the flour, sugar, brown sugar, baking powder, salt, and cinnamon in a bowl. After mixing well, make a depression in the middle of the bowl. Add the egg, melted butter, and milk in the well. Stir until just combined. Fold in the raspberries. Fill each muffin cup about ¾ full.
- To make the topping, combine the rum, lime juice, and powdered sugar into a syrupy liquid. Spoon the mixture equally over the batter in each muffin cup.
- Mix the chopped walnuts, brown sugar, cinnamon, and flour in a small bowl until well blended. Pour the melted butter over the nut mixture and stir. Add 1 spoonful or so over the batter in each muffin cup.
- Bake for 25 minutes.
- To make a glaze, combine ½ cup powdered sugar and 3 tablespoons lime juice. Pour the glaze over the muffins at serving time.

The Lady Goodwood
Bed & Breakfast

*I*n 1895, James Hanson, a prominent businessman and local grocer, built this elegant three-story Queen Anne home, complete with parquet floors, pocket doors, wrap-around porch with a magnificent river view, and stained and etched glass windows. Innkeepers Susan and Nick Chaves "fell in love with this home the instant we walked through the front door, and couldn't wait to share it with our guests," Susan said. She, Nick, and Susan's parents now own and operate the bed-and-breakfast, having "pooled our skills and efforts to completely restore the house in the Victorian style. We opened for business on September 1, 1996." They offer three guestrooms at the Lady Goodwood.

On the banks of the St. Croix, a National Wild and Scenic River, Stillwater is a popular draw for visitors. Just three blocks from the inn, a staircase descends the river bluff to Main Street and its ancient caves, sidewalk cafés, elegant restaurants, gift and antique shops, used and rare book stores, art galleries, and nightspots. Other attractions in and around Stillwater include a dinner train, a jazz dinner cruise on a paddleboat, museums, canoeing or kayaking, hot air balloon rides, live theater, beautiful Victorian architecture, and several state parks.

The Lady Goodwood Bed & Breakfast
704 First Street South
Stillwater, MN 55082
612-439-3771

Grandmother's Strawberry Muffins

"This is my grandmother's recipe," writes Innkeeper Susan Chaves. "As a child, I always looked forward to picking berries from her garden to prepare these muffins." Makes 18 muffins.

> ½ cup butter or margarine, softened
> 1 cup sugar
> 1 teaspoon vanilla extract
> 1 tablespoon lemon juice
> 3 eggs
> 2 cups flour
> ½ teaspoon salt
> ¾ teaspoon cream of tartar
> ½ teaspoon baking soda
> ½ cup nonfat sour cream
> 1 cup fresh or frozen strawberries, puréed

Frosting
> 1 cup powdered sugar
> 1 teaspoon vanilla
> 2 teaspoons milk
> 1 tablespoon lemon zest

- Preheat oven to 350 degrees. Grease muffin cups.
- With an electric mixer, beat the softened butter or margarine, sugar, vanilla, and lemon juice until fluffy. Add the eggs, 1 at a time.
- In a separate bowl, sift together the flour, salt, cream of tartar, and baking soda.
- In another bowl, mix the sour cream with the puréed strawberries.
- Alternately fold the flour mixture and strawberry mixture into the egg mixture.
- Fill greased muffin cups ¾ full.
- Bake for 20 to 25 minutes.
- Combine powdered sugar, vanilla, milk, and lemon zest to make frosting. Drizzle frosting on cooled muffins.

Watch Hill Bed & Breakfast

*W*hen guests come to Barbara Lauterbach's bed-and-breakfast, they may come for many reasons — but when they come back, "food" is always one that draws them.

A gourmet chef, Barbara trained at renowned culinary institutes in Paris, Italy, and England. Her long food-related career has included developing cooking schools for a chain of department stores, serving as an instructor at the New England Culinary Institute, and acting as a consultant and spokesperson for food-related businesses. She also has done regular television cooking segments and presents classes around the country. When she bought the B&B in 1989, her food background was just one of the talents that made innkeeping attractive to her. Guests love to sit and chat during an excellent breakfast, and Barbara holds cooking classes at the B&B.

Watch Hill is one of the oldest homes in Centre Harbor. Built circa 1772 by the brother of the town's founder, it has views of Lake Winnipesaukee, just down the street from the home. Guests in the four guestrooms especially enjoy the home's porch in the summer or warming up with a mug of hot cider after skiing or snowmobiling in the winter.

Barbara's full country breakfast often showcases New Hampshire products and may feature fresh, hot breads, sausage, bacon, home-fries, fresh fruit, and brown eggs. Guests enjoy the food and the conversation, which often turns to the how her B&B was named (after the champion bull mastiffs Barbara used to raise from the Watch Hill kennel in Cincinnati, Ohio).

Watch Hill Bed & Breakfast
P.O. Box 1605
Center Harbor, NH 03226
603-253-4334

Harvest Fruit Muffins

Innkeeper Barbara Lauterbach suggests to save time and serve these muffins freshly-baked in the morning, mix the dry ingredients together, then mix the topping in a separate bowl, the night before. Mix together and blend in the liquids in the morning, just before baking. "Guests are eager to be punctual for breakfast," she notes, "when they are enticed downstairs by the fragrance of these muffins baking." Makes 12 muffins.

- 2 cups flour
- ½ cup sugar
- 2 teaspoons baking powder
- ½ teaspoon baking soda
- ½ teaspoon salt
- ½ teaspoon cinnamon
- ½ teaspoon nutmeg, freshly ground
- 1 egg
- ½ cup oil
- ⅓ cup milk
- 1 8-ounce container peach yogurt
- ¾ cup dried fruit, chopped

Topping
- 3 tablespoons flour
- 2 tablespoons brown sugar
- 3 tablespoons nuts, chopped
- ½ teaspoon cinnamon
- 2 tablespoons butter or margarine, softened

- Preheat oven to 400 degrees. Lightly grease muffin cups.
- Combine flour, sugar, baking powder, baking soda, salt, cinnamon, and nutmeg in a large bowl. Set aside.
- In a medium bowl, beat the egg; add the oil, milk, yogurt, and dried fruit, and combine. Add the egg mixture to the flour mixture, stirring gently just until moistened. Do not overbeat.
- To make the topping, combine the flour, brown sugar, chopped nuts, cinnamon, and butter or margarine.
- Fill muffin cups ⅔ full, and spoon 1 heaping tablespoon of topping over the batter.
- Bake for 20 minutes, checking at 15 minutes.

The Inn at Ludington

*I*nnkeeper Diane Shields knew many innkeepers and their inns before she entered into the business herself. She owned and operated a reservation service, and she first saw the 1889 Queen Anne Victorian mansion when she came to visit innkeepers in Ludington.

"When I found out it was for sale, I decided to pursue my dream of full-time innkeeping, and within three months had moved in, lock, stock, and barrel." The three-story home has six guestrooms, to which Diane added bathrooms and redecorated after purchasing the inn in 1990.

Guests at the inn can explore the area beaches, golf courses, or hop on the Lake Michigan car ferry. Or they might enjoy relaxing, reading, talking, or playing board games by the fireplace in the spacious parlor. Diane's homemade breakfast is served in the formal dining room, but is an informal, fun affair.

In addition to innkeeping, Diane conducts seminars for aspiring innkeepers, and writes regularly for bed-and-breakfast newsletters and magazines. She is a columnist for *The Inn Times*.

The Inn at Ludington
701 East Ludington Avenue
Ludington, MI 49431
616-845-7055

Jane's Double-Good Michigan Blueberry Muffins

"My friend Jane Grey, who is the food editor at our local paper where I also work, gave me this recipe," writes Innkeeper Diane Shields. "Jane says when she makes them, she places the blueberries individually into the muffins, so there are no arguments over who got more blueberries." This recipe also does double duty as a coffee cake. Simply spread in a greased, round, 9-inch pan, sprinkle with cinnamon-sugar, and bake. It can also be doubled and baked in a 13-inch pan. "See why it's double good?" Makes 14 muffins.

- 2 cups flour
- ⅓ cup sugar
- 3 teaspoons baking powder
- 1 teaspoon cinnamon, ginger, nutmeg, or allspice, optional
- 1 cup milk
- ⅓ cup oil
- 1 egg
- 1 cup fresh or frozen blueberries

- Preheat oven to 400 degrees. Grease muffin cups.
- Sift together the flour, sugar, baking powder, and cinnamon (or ginger, nutmeg, or allspice) into a large bowl.
- In a separate bowl, mix the milk, oil, and egg; add to the flour mixture. Fold in the blueberries.
- Spoon batter into greased muffin cups.
- Bake for 20 minutes.

Diantha's Garden Bed & Breakfast

*H*omemade breakfasts are a highlight of guests' stay here, and muffins are one of Innkeeper Linda Cooper's specialties. Diantha's Garden is a dream-come-true for Linda and Jim Cooper. Jim is native of Southamptom, "while Linda has lived in town for only 31 years," they joke.

Their bed-and-breakfast is named for Diantha Coe Clapp, wife of Farmer Taylor Clapp. This eighteenth-century farmhouse is located on several acres in a still-rural setting. Diantha Clapp lived on this land from 1846 until 1885 or 1886. The perennial gardens are named in honor of her.

In addition to the spacious grounds, guests may relax in a comfortable large living room, a sitting room on a cool screened porch. Two guestrooms feature heirlooms from both Linda's and Jim's families, as well as treasures collected over the years by Linda.

Diantha's Garden is accessible to many Western Massachusetts points of interest, such as "Five Colleges," the Basketball Hall of Fame, Yankee Candle Company, Historic Old Deerfield, and the Mount Tom Ski Area. Sturbridge Village and the Stockbridge/Lenox areas are only one hour away.

Diantha's Garden Bed & Breakfast
20 Wolcott Road
Southampton, MA 01073
413-529-0093
Fax 413-529-0456

Key Lime Muffins

Reminiscent of Linda's native Florida, these muffins are a summer treat with fresh fruit, as well as a bright treat on cold winter mornings. Makes 12 muffins.

- ¼ cup butter, softened
- ½ cup sugar
- 2 eggs
- ¼ cup Key (or regular) lime juice
- 1½ teaspoons lime zest
- 1 teaspoon baking soda
- 1 8-ounce container Key lime or plain yogurt
- 2 cups flour
- ⅛ teaspoon salt

Glaze

juice of 1 lime
sugar

- Preheat oven to 375 degrees. Spray muffin cups well with nonstick cooking spray.
- Cream together well the butter and sugar. Add the eggs, 1 at a time, then mix in the juice and zest.
- Add the baking soda to the yogurt, and set aside.
- In a separate bowl, mix the flour and salt, and add to the butter mixture. Then add the yogurt mixture. Batter may be stiff; don't overmix.
- Spoon into muffin cups.
- Bake for 18 to 20 minutes.
- While the muffins are still warm, dip the tops in lime juice and then in sugar.

The Beazley House
Bed & Breakfast Inn

*J*im and Carol Beazley gave up careers — he was a photojournalist and she a registered nurse — to open Beazley House in 1981 as Napa's first bed-and-breakfast inn. "Some of our friends thought we were nuts," says Carol, "but the only thing we were afraid of was not getting the chance to try." The mansion they found is in old Napa, just a stroll from shopping and fine restaurants. Napa is only an hour north of San Francisco at the southern gateway of the world-famous Napa Valley wine country. It is a tree-shaded, river city surrounded by vineyards and wineries. Within minutes of the inn are wine touring, ballooning, cycling, hot mud baths, and mineral spas.

The Beazley House sits on half an acre of lawns and gardens. Visitors will see why it has been a Napa landmark since 1902 with its verdant lawns and bright flowers and welcoming stained glass front door. Elegant yet comfortable, the sitting room is to the left, and the beautiful gardens can be seen through the French doors straight ahead. The guestrooms are large and individually decorated with beautiful antiques and queen-sized beds. The Carriage House, nestled among gardens and tall trees behind the mansion, is the "country side" of the inn. In it, five charming, generous rooms with private spas and fireplaces await guests' discovery.

For breakfast, Beazley House serves a delicious buffet of fresh-baked muffins, crustless quiche, a variety of fresh fruits with yogurt, sweet orange juice, and a selection of teas and steaming coffee. Innkeepers Jim and Carol Beazley specialize in tasty, low-fat cuisine that pleases their guests.

The Beazley House
Bed & Breakfast Inn
1910 First Street
Napa, CA 94559
707-257-1649

Mandarin Orange Muffins

These moist muffins will delight orange-lovers with triple orange flavor. Try them on a gray winter day for a hint of the tropics! Makes 24 muffins.

5 cups unbleached flour
⅔ cup sugar
1 teaspoon baking powder
2 teaspoons baking soda
2 teaspoons cinnamon
2 12-ounce cans mandarin oranges, including juice
2 eggs
2 egg whites
2 tablespoons oil
1 teaspoon orange zest
½ teaspoon orange extract
  sugar

- Preheat oven to 325 degrees. Spray muffin cups with nonstick cooking spray.
- Mix together flour, sugar, baking powder, baking soda, and cinnamon so all are blended thoroughly.
- In a measuring pitcher, combine the mandarin oranges, eggs, egg whites, oil, orange zest, and orange extract. Pinch the pieces of orange apart, so there are no large clumps. Pour orange-egg mixture into flour mixture, and mix just until moist. Do not overmix.
- Spoon batter into muffin cups, and sprinkle about ¼ teaspoon of sugar on top of each.
- Bake for about 20 minutes or until golden brown.

The Inn at Maplewood Farm

*L*aura and Jayme Simoes left busy lives working in a metropolitan public relations firm for life literally along a slow lane. They purchased this bucolic, picture-perfect New England farmhouse and entered careers as innkeepers. Their inn, which has welcomed visitors for two hundred years, sits back from a winding country road, just a short drive from the town of Hillsborough. Located on fourteen acres, guests looking for a quiet getaway are delighted to find the nearest neighbors are a few cows and the 1,400-acre Fox State Forest.

Laura, who also has a food-writing background, prepares dynamite breakfasts, served in the sunny dining room downstairs. While enjoying the fireplace or rocking on the porch are the chosen daytime pursuits of many guests, there is plenty to do in the area. Laura and Jayme love directing guests to little-known antique stores, historic villages, picnic spots and waterfalls, all within a few minutes' drive.

The Inn's four guestrooms are decorated in antiques, including an antique radio at bedside in each. Jayme's infatuation with the Golden Age of Radio has led to his own transmitter on the farm, from which he broadcasts old-time radio programs to the guestrooms via the vintage radios. Request a favorite and, chances are, he's got it in this 1,000-plus show collection.

The Inn at Maplewood Farm
P.O. Box 1478
447 Center Road
Hillsborough, NH 03224
603-464-4242
Toll-free 800-644-6695

Maplewood Nut Muffins

"Here is a favorite muffin recipe," writes Innkeeper Laura Simoes. "Even after years of baking muffins, these still tempt me!" Makes 12 to 18 medium, 36 mini, or 8 giant muffins.

2 cups flour
¼ cup sugar
1 tablespoon baking powder
½ teaspoon salt
1 egg
1 cup milk
½ cup butter, softened
⅔ cup New Hampshire maple syrup
2 teaspoons maple extract
1 cup pecans, hazelnuts, or walnuts, chopped

■ Preheat oven to 350 degrees. Line muffin pan with paper liners or spray with nonstick cooking spray.
■ In a medium bowl, mix the flour, sugar, baking powder, and salt.
■ Add the egg, milk, butter, maple syrup, maple extract, and chopped nuts. Mix just until blended.
■ Bake for 20 minutes, or until tops spring back when touched. Serve warm.

Good Medicine Lodge

*W*hen Susan Ridder, formerly an executive with a large hotel chain, and Christopher Ridder, formerly a travel agent, decided to open a bed-and-breakfast, they got as far as Whitefish, Montana, before finding the perfect place. Their Good Medicine Lodge originally opened with three guestrooms and then added a six-room addition in 1993. It has since received rave reviews and praise for its ambiance, attention to detail, healthy breakfasts, and environmental policies.

The lodge is built of cedar timbers and has "a rustic and informal atmosphere, where guests can feel at home," Chris said. Most of the rooms and suites have balconies and mountain views, and they all have custom-made lodgepole beds and vaulted wood ceilings. Decorated in a Western motif, the roomy interiors are punctuated by roaring fireplaces and fabrics influenced by Native American textiles. Each morning, guests indulge in a European-style buffet that includes fresh-baked muffins, cobblers and breads, fruits, cereals and granola, yogurt, and sliced meats and cheeses. A hearty breakfast is essential for many of the lodge's guests who come to ski or fish or pursue a variety of outdoor activities. Chris and Susan, outdoor enthusiasts themselves, have put in a ski room with boot and glove dryers, as well as an outdoor spa to soak weary muscles.

The ski lifts at Big Mountain resort are six miles from the inn, and summer travelers enjoy gondola rides and mountain biking trails there. Glacier National Park, only 24 miles away, offers more options. The beach and boating and fishing at Whitefish Lake are only a half-mile away, and Flathead Lake is a thirty-minute drive.

Good Medicine Lodge is a member of the Green Hotels Association and asks guests to recycle when possible, and Chris and Susan follow environmentally-sensitive operations procedures.

Good Medicine Lodge

537 Wisconsin Avenue
Whitefish, MT 59937
406-862-5488
Fax 406-862-5489

Melba Muffins

These moist muffins are often part of the breakfast buffet at Good Medicine Lodge. Makes 12 muffins.

$\frac{1}{2}$ cup sour cream, room temperature
$\frac{1}{3}$ cup peach juice, room temperature
2 ounces butter, melted and cooled
1 egg, room temperature
1$\frac{1}{2}$ teaspoons vanilla extract
$\frac{1}{4}$ teaspoon orange rind, grated
2 cups flour
1 cup sugar
1 teaspoon baking powder
1 teaspoon baking soda
$\frac{1}{2}$ teaspoon salt
1 cup fresh peaches, chopped
1 cup fresh or frozen raspberries

- Preheat oven to 400 degrees. Line muffin pan with paper liners, and spray top of pan with nonstick cooking spray.
- In a large bowl, blend the sour cream, peach juice, butter, egg, vanilla, and orange rind.
- Add the flour, sugar, baking powder, baking soda, and salt to the sour cream mixture.
- Stir in the peaches and raspberries.
- Spoon batter into muffin cups.
- Bake for 20 to 25 minutes.

The Inn at the Round Barn Farm

*I*n the heart of Vermont amidst 85 acres of mountains, meadows, and ponds is the Inn at the Round Barn Farm, which gets its name from the 12-sided barn built in 1910 and now fully restored. Until the 1960s, this was a working dairy farm. Then, Jack and Doreen Simko and their daughter AnneMarie DeFreest converted the nineteenth-century farmhouse and attached horse barn to guestrooms, common spaces, and a cross-country ski center. The round barn is now used for large gatherings, and in the lower level is a sixty-foot indoor lap pool that extends into a greenhouse.

The inn offers 11 guestrooms, all with original pine floors. The first floor includes a library with a wood-burning fireplace, a good selection of coffeetable books about Vermont, and a decanter of sherry. In the lower level is a game room with an antique pool table, an organ, and many modern-day diversions such as a VCR. Breakfast, served in a sunny room with a view of the hills, includes juice, fresh fruit, muffins, and a daily hot entrée.

The inn has thirty kilometers of groomed cross-country ski trails and offers guests rentals — including snowshoe rentals. In the wintertime, downhill skiing is just a few minutes away, and the inn is beautifully decorated and lit for the holidays. In the summertime, the inn hosts concerts and art exhibits, and is an ideal gathering place for large groups.

The Inn at the Round Barn Farm
R.R. Box 247
East Warren Road
Waitsfield, VT 05673
802-496-2276
Fax 802-496-8832

Morning Glory Muffins

"Always loved by guests, these wonderful morning muffins are hearty yet light. When they are served with a flavored butter or whipped cream cheese, nobody can pass them up!" warns AnneMarie DeFreest. Makes 24 muffins.

   3 eggs
   ¾ cup oil
   2 teaspoons vanilla extract
   ½ cup low-fat milk
   2 cups flour
   ½ cup bran cereal
   1 cup sugar
   2 teaspoons baking soda
   2 teaspoons cinnamon
   2 cups carrots, grated
   ½ cup raisins
   ½ cup nuts, chopped
   ½ cup coconut
   ½ cup apple, peeled and grated

- Preheat oven to 350 degrees. Grease muffin cups.
- Beat together the eggs, oil, vanilla, and milk.
- In a separate bowl, combine the flour, bran cereal, sugar, baking soda, and cinnamon. Add the carrots, raisins, nuts, coconut, and apple.
- Slowly add the mixtures together until just combined. Pour into greased muffin cups, filling full.
- Bake for 20 minutes.

Red Shutters

*R*ed Shutters, a cozy bed-and-breakfast that caters to non-smokers, is located in a quiet, residential neighborhood, a five-minute walk to ocean beach, shops, and restaurants. Within a short drive are historic sites, outlet shopping, antique shops, and Maine's scenic villages and rocky coastline.

The inn offers three guestrooms, and is open in the summertime. Innkeepers Gil and Evelyn Billings also run Lupine House Bed-and-Breakfast, in Florence, Massachusetts, from fall to spring.

The homemade breakfast includes hot-from-the-oven muffins, fresh seasonal fruit, granola, assorted juices, and hot beverages.

Red Shutters

7 Cross Street
York Beach, ME 03910
207-363-6292
Toll-free 800-890-9766

Orange Chocolate Chip Muffins

This unusual combination of flavors often has guests reaching for seconds. Makes 12 muffins.

>   2 medium-sized oranges, well scrubbed and wiped dry
>   3/4 cup sugar
>   2 tablespoons olive oil
>   3 egg whites
>   1/2 cup fresh orange juice
>   1/2 cup plain yogurt
> 1 1/4 cups flour
>   3/4 cup oat bran
>   1 teaspoon baking powder
>   1/2 teaspoon baking soda
>   4 ounces semi-sweet chocolate chips
>   sugar

- Preheat oven to 400 degrees. Spray muffin cups with nonstick cooking spray.
- Peel the oranges, removing and discarding as much of the white pith from the peel as possible. Grate the orange rind, and set aside.
- In a large bowl using a wooden spoon, beat the sugar and olive oil. Add the egg whites; beat until just mixed. Add the orange rind, orange juice, and yogurt, mixing thoroughly.
- In a separate bowl, mix the flour, oat bran, baking powder, and baking soda. Add the flour mixture to the orange juice mixture, gently blending. Blend in the chocolate chips.
- Fill each muffin cup 3/4 full. Sprinkle the top of the muffin batter with sugar.
- Bake for 20 minutes, or until golden brown.

Garth Woodside Mansion
Bed & Breakfast Country Inn

*O*n the National Register of Historic Places, the Garth Woodside Mansion still looks much as it did when the Garth family resided at "Woodside," which was built in 1871 as a summer home for John and Helen Garth. Colonel Garth, whose local business interests included both tobacco and lumber, was at that time one of Hannibal's more prominent citizens. Mark Twain wrote, "I spent many nights with John and Helen Garth in their spacious, beautiful home. They were children with me and afterwards schoolmates."

The mansion is set among noble old trees on 39 acres of meadows, woodlands, and gardens. Inside, the home is trimmed with walnut woodwork and decorated with Victorian antiques. The inn is conveniently located to all of Hannibal's attractions: the boyhood home of Mark Twain, theaters, riverboat rides, caves, restaurants, sightseeing tours, and more.

Diane and Irv Feinberg spent two years searching for the perfect B&B property. Being lovers of the Victorian era, they wanted a home where the original detail remained. Here, they have been fortunate to acquire many of the home's original furnishings. "In 1988, we started the restoration and opened the inn," Irv said. Four years later, their home was chosen from two hundred entries for the National Historic Trust's "Great American Home" award. They have since opened Abigail's Secret, a romantic hideway in the historic district of Hannibal. Made just for two, Abigail's Secret has a sunken two-person whirlpool, a canopy bed, and other surprises. Guests who wander downtown can have their Victorian portrait taken at the Feinberg's old-time photo studio, Somewhere in Time.

Garth Woodside Mansion Bed & Breakfast Country Inn
Rural Route 3
Hannibal, MO 63401
573-221-2789

Orange Marmalade Muffins

Innkeeper Diane Feinberg looked forward to visiting her grandmother, in part because Diane would be treated to these special muffins the first morning of the visit. Diane admits she even savored them at other times of the day, sometimes even getting caught. Makes 12 muffins.

  2 cups flour
  ¼ cup sugar
  1 tablespoon baking powder
  ½ teaspoon salt
  1 egg
  1 cup milk
  3 tablespoons butter or margarine, melted
  2 teaspoons orange rind, grated
  ⅓ cup orange marmalade

- Preheat oven to 400 degrees. Grease muffin cups.
- In a large bowl, stir together the flour, sugar, baking powder, and salt.
- In a separate bowl, beat the egg with the milk, melted butter, and orange rind. Add the egg mixture to the flour mixture, stirring only until flour is moistened.
- Fill greased 2½-inch muffin pan ½ full. To each muffin cup, add about 1 teaspoon of marmalade. Use remaining batter to fill pan ⅔ full.
- Bake until well browned, about 20 to 25 minutes. Serve warm.

Inn at Gristmill Square

*S*ince 1771, a mill has been on the site of Warm Spring Run, in the heart of Warm Springs, Virginia. The present mill was erected in 1900 and operated until 1970, when it became the home of the Waterwheel Restaurant located on the grounds of the inn. The building is now listed as a National and Virginia Historic Landmark.

The Inn at Gristmill Square was created in 1972, utilizing five original nineteenth century buildings. The old blacksmith shop houses the Country Store and office; the hardware store is now space for seven guest units; the Steel House, once a private home, has four guestrooms; and the old Miller House also has guestrooms. (The restaurant is the fifth building.) The inn offers a Bath and Tennis Club with three tennis courts, a swimming pool, and sauna. Nearby are golf courses, horseback riding, fishing, hunting, and hiking.

Inn at Gristmill Square
Box 359
Warm Springs, VA 24484
540-839-2231
Fax 540-839-5770

Orange Nut Muffins

"Each morning at the Inn at Gristmill Square, we deliver a picnic basket to the door of each guest," writes Innkeeper Janice McWilliams. "In the basket is a continental break-fast that includes, among other things, muffins that we bake each morning. I have one favorite basic recipe that I am always adapting to fit the weather, time of year, or just my mood. Below are three variations." Makes 12 medium muffins.

¾ cup orange juice
1 egg, beaten
¼ cup canola oil
2 cups flour
½ cup sugar
1 tablespoon baking powder
¼ teaspoon salt
  grated rind of 1 orange
½ cup pecans, chopped

- Preheat oven to 375 degrees. Spray muffin cups with nonstick cooking spray.
- In a large bowl, combine orange juice, egg, and oil.
- In a separate bowl, sift the flour, sugar, baking powder, and salt together; combine with orange juice mixture just until moist. Stir in the orange rind and chopped pecans. Be careful not to over mix; the batter will be lumpy.
- Spoon batter into muffin cups.
- Bake for 25 minutes or until top is firm.

Variation: Cranberry Walnut Muffins
Substitute milk for the orange juice. Add ½ bag of fresh, chopped cranberries and ½ cup chopped English walnuts to the batter. Also add ½ teaspoon of nutmeg, optional. Omit the orange rind and chopped pecans.

Variation: Apple Raisin Muffins
Substitute milk for the orange juice. Chop 1 apple in a food processor. Add ½ cup raisins to the batter along with 1 teaspoon of cinnamon. Sprinkle the chopped apple on top of the muffin batter. Omit the orange rind and chopped pecans.

Allen House Victorian Inn

*F*eatured in travel guides and feature stories, the Allen House Victorian Inn is located in the heart of Amherst, Massachusetts, on over three landscaped acres. Built in 1886 by Lysander H. Allen, a local wire goods manufacturer, the home features many peaked gables, an ornately carved Austrian vergeboard, oriental Chippendale and multiple- relief shingles, all making it one of the finest examples of Queen Anne and Stick-style architecture in the area. Innkeepers Ann and Alan Zieminski restored the interior "to reflect the Aesthetic Movement, the Victorian subculture that emphasized art in the interior decor," Alan said. The original hand-carved cherry fireplace mantels are cataloged by the Metropolitan Museum of Art in New York City.

This 18-room inn offers seven spacious guestrooms, a full formal breakfast, and afternoon and evening tea. Guests are within walking distance of the Emily Dickinson Homestead, Amherst College, the University of Massachusetts, art galleries, museums, bookstores, theaters, concerts, shops, and restaurants. Also nearby is Mount Holyoke, Smith and Hampshire Colleges, Northampton, Yankee Candle Company, Norman Rockwell Museum, Historic Deerfield, and Old Sturbridge Village.

Allen House Victorian Inn
599 Main Street
Amherst, MA 01002
413-253-5000

Orange Pumpkin Nut Muffins

Fall is the most popular season in Western Massachusetts, with its beautiful foliage. Part of fall is the pumpkin harvest, so these muffins seem to be a natural for the table at the Allen House. Makes 15 to 18 muffins.

1 egg
¾ cup milk
¼ cup oil
1¾ cups flour
½ cup sugar
2 teaspoons baking powder
1 teaspoon salt
1 cup canned pumpkin
1 seedless orange, cut into slices, and rind pulverized in food processor
1 teaspoon cinnamon
1 teaspoon nutmeg

Topping
1 cup brown sugar
1 teaspoon flour
1 cup nuts, chopped

- Preheat oven to 400 degrees. Line muffin pan with paper liners or spray with nonstick cooking spray.
- In a large bowl, beat egg, and stir in milk and oil. Mix in flour, sugar, baking powder, salt, pumpkin, orange slices, pulverized orange rind, cinnamon, and nutmeg. The batter will be slightly lumpy.
- Pour the batter into muffin cups.
- To make topping, combine the brown sugar, flour, and chopped nuts. Spoon over the top of each muffin.
- Bake for 20 to 25 minutes, or until golden brown.

Walnut Street Inn

*I*nnkeepers Paula and Gary Blankenship returned to their Ozark roots after 15 years of climbing corporate ladders and living in five major cities across the United States. As their daughter approached school age, they decided it was time to put down roots and go home to Springfield, Missouri. Walnut Street Historic District provided the urban feel they had grown used to: shops, restaurants, art galleries, and theaters, plus the Southwest Missouri State University campus is within walking distance. The Walnut Street Inn provided the peaceful oasis they sought.

The Inn, built in 1894, is listed as a National Historic Site, and it features Corinthian columns on its airy veranda, gleaming hardwood floors, and antique furnishings. Each of the 12 guestrooms has a unique "personality." Guests can treat themselves to a relaxing soak in a double whirlpool tub, toast their toes by a fireplace, and sleep under a soft feather comforter. The Blankenships and their staff enjoy helping their guests make their visit memorable, from helping with dinner reservations to offering homemade cookies.

Sumptuous breakfasts that feature Ozark specialties, such as oatmeal-black walnut pancakes and these muffins, are served on the Inn's collection of heirloom china. Guests can pull up an antique chair and enjoy the conversation during breakfast in the dining room, or they can pamper themselves with breakfast delivered to their room.

Walnut Street Inn
900 East Walnut
Springfield, MO 65806
417-864-6346

Ozark Persimmon Muffins

When persimmons are in season, Paula and Gary Blankenship add these delicious muffins to their breakfast fare. Makes 12 muffins.

- ½ cup persimmon pulp (about 2 seeded and peeled persimmons)
- 1 egg, beaten
- ½ cup milk
- ¼ cup butter, melted
- 1½ cups flour
- ½ cup sugar
- 3 teaspoons baking powder
- ½ teaspoon cinnamon
- 1 teaspoon nutmeg
- ¼ teaspoon ground cloves

- Preheat oven to 400 degrees.
- In a medium mixing bowl, beat the persimmon pulp, egg, milk, and butter until smooth.
- In a separate, larger bowl, mix together the flour, sugar, cinnamon, nutmeg, and cloves. Stir the persimmon mixture into the flour mixture just until moistened. The batter will be lumpy.
- Spoon the batter into ungreased muffin cups.
- Bake for 15 to 18 minutes, or until golden.

Windyledge Bed & Breakfast

*D*ick and Susan Vogts' Windyledge overlooks the Merrimack Valley, with New Hampshire's White Mountains beyond. The hilltop colonial is a cozy retreat, featuring oriental rugs, family antiques, and comfortable country furnishings. Guests are invited to enjoy a glass of wine and a fireside chat, play the piano, swim in the pool, putter in the garden, feed the horse, or lounge on the deck.

Dick and Susan started innkeeping in 1990. These days, Dick's gourmet recipes are a perfect way for guests to start their days, with "honey 'n spice blueberry pancakes," ricotta souffle with raspberry sauce, apricot-glazed French toast and, of course, homemade muffins and jams.

Dick retired in 1992 from his corporate career in distribution and planning. Susan still works part-time as a dental receptionist. They built Windyledge in 1973, and raised four children. When the last went off to college, they opened the B&B.

Windyledge Bed & Breakfast
1264 Hatfield Road
Hopkinton, NH 03229
603-746-4054
Fax 603-746-4052

Peach Cobbler Muffins

Innkeeper Dick Vogt recommends that this recipe be used only when it is peach season. "You come home from the fruit stand with some fresh peaches and bite into one that is wonderful . . . as only peaches can be. Then set aside two large ones and do yourself a favor and makes these muffins. With ripe peaches, this recipe is sensational." Makes 12 muffins.

   1 jumbo egg
   ½ cup sour cream
   ½ cup milk
   1 teaspoon pure vanilla extract
   3 tablespoons oil
   2 large fresh, ripe peaches, peeled and diced
   2 cups flour
   ½ cup sugar
   1 tablespoon baking powder
   ¼ teaspoon baking soda
   ¼ teaspoon salt

Topping
   1 tablespoon butter, melted
   2 tablespoons flour
   2 tablespoons sugar
   ⅛ teaspoon cinnamon

■ Preheat oven to 375 degrees. Grease muffin cups.
■ Beat the egg, sour cream, milk, vanilla, and oil, and set aside. Prepare the peaches, and fold them into the egg mixture.
■ In a separate bowl, mix the flour, sugar, baking powder, baking soda, and salt. Combine flour mixture with peach mixture.
■ Spoon batter into muffin cups.
■ To make topping, combine the melted butter with the flour, sugar, and cinnamon. Sprinkle the topping on top of the muffin batter.
■ Bake for 26 minutes.

Wild Swan Inn

*B*uilt around the turn of the century, Wild Swan is a classic example of Queen Anne-style Victorian architecture, with its ornate gingerbread and fancy finials perched on its rooftops. Painted a deep pink with green and burgundy accents, this home is typical of an age of architectural excess popular on seaside homes erected in Lewes during the heyday of the industrial era.

Hope and Michael Tyler, who operate Wild Swan, are self-proclaimed old house addicts. They restored an 1880s country home in northern Delaware where they lived for 25 years. After raising four children, they decided to settle in the quiet town of Lewes, the first town in the First State. They left careers in public relations (Michael) and state government (Hope) when they began innkeeping in January 1993.

The Tylers' antique collections include quilts, swans, door stops, and cameras. Michael enjoys playing wax cylinder records on an authentic Edison phonograph. Guests may also enjoy one of Michael's player piano concerts.

Wild Swan is within walking distance of the downtown historic district, where guests find fine antiques, handcrafted gifts, and restaurants. Lewes Beach is a little more than a mile from the inn, and Cape Henlopen State Park is only minutes away by car or one of the inn's complimentary bicycles. The state park has 4,000 acres of clean beaches, nature trails, high dunes, and a World War II observation tower.

Wild Swan Inn

525 Kings Highway
Lewes, DE 19958
302-645-8550

Peach of a Tomato Muffins

Innkeeper Mike Tyler created this unusual recipe that always pleasantly surprises guests. "When I was in high school, I had a friend who mixed fresh peaches and tomatoes — nothing else — as a tasty summer salad," Mike said. "So I tried this combo in a muffin recipe and it worked great!" Makes 12 muffins.

2	cups flour
1/2	teaspoon salt
1/2	teaspoon baking soda
1/2	teaspoon baking powder
1/2	cup egg substitute
1/2	cup brown sugar
3/4	cup oil
1	teaspoon vanilla extract
3/4	cup tomato, chopped
3/4	cup fresh peaches, chopped
1/3	cup poppy seeds
1 1/2	teaspoons cinnamon
1 1/2	teaspoons ground ginger
1	cup walnuts, coarsely chopped

- Preheat oven to 400 degrees. Grease muffin cups.
- Sift together the flour, salt, baking soda, and baking powder.
- In a separate, large bowl, combine egg substitute, brown sugar, oil, and vanilla. Add the tomatoes and peaches, poppy seeds, cinnamon, and ginger. Stir in the flour mixture, mixing gently until all ingredients are moist. Fold in the chopped walnuts.
- Spoon batter into greased muffin cups. Fill almost to the top.
- Bake for 25 minutes.

Grant Corner Inn

*B*reakfast is such a special event at Santa Fe's Grant Corner Inn that it is open to the public by reservation. Innkeeper Louise Stewart has earned a great reputation for the inn's food, as well as the 12 guestrooms. How good is breakfast? So good that Louise's Grant Corner Inn cookbook is a best seller among guests who want to take a breakfast home with them!

Louise was born into an innkeeping family, and she's continued the tradition, raising her daughter, "Bumpy," at the inn. Louise's husband, Pat Walter, transformed a three-story Colonial home, right in downtown Santa Fe, into a romantic inn, complete with white picket fence and gazebo. It took nine long months of major renovation before the inn opened in 1982.

The home was built for the Winsor family, whose photo, among others of the home's residents over the years, hangs in the hallway. The dining rooms and parlor are on the first floor, with guestrooms on the second and third floors. The decor includes Louise's collection of antiques, Indian art, and bunnies (every type except the live kind), which have multiplied wildly and are everywhere, from tea pots and napkin rings to door stops.

Grant Corner Inn

122 Grant Avenue
Santa Fe, NM 87501
505-983-6678

Peanut Butter Bran Muffins

Creative flavor combinations are often on the breakfast table at the Grant Corner Inn, and this is one of guests' favorites. Makes 12 muffins.

1 cup flour
⅓ cup light brown sugar, packed
2 teaspoons baking powder
½ teaspoon salt
¼ teaspoon baking soda
1 egg, beaten
1 cup sour cream
3 tablespoons oil
1 cup bran cereal
½ cup chunky peanut butter
2 tablespoons honey

- Preheat oven to 400 degrees. Line muffin pan with paper liners.
- In a medium bowl, combine the flour, brown sugar, baking powder, salt, and baking soda; set aside.
- In a small bowl, mix the egg, sour cream, and oil; stir in the bran cereal and let stand for 5 minutes. Add the peanut butter and honey, stirring to mix thoroughly.
- Stir bran-peanut butter mixture into the flour mixture until just blended; do not overmix.
- Fill muffin cups ⅔ full.
- Bake for 20 to 25 minutes, or until tops spring back when lightly touched.

L'Auberge Provençale

*B*uilt in 1753 and known as Mt. Airy, this farmhouse has watched soldiers from both the Revolutionary and Civil Wars pass by. Today, the main house and cottages are known as L'Auberge Provençale, a highly-acclaimed French country inn and restaurant.

Alain and Celeste Borel found this farmhouse from the air, in Alain's small plane. They were living and working in Key West, but they wanted their own full-service inn in which Alain could specialize in cuisine from his native Provençe. Alain is a fourth-generation master chef who began his career by peeling potatoes for his great-grandfather's hotel at age six. Since then, he had worked as a chef in Montreal, Vermont, Seattle, and Key West before opening the inn with four guestrooms and a restaurant in 1981. After several additions, including one to their family, a son, the Borels now have ten guestrooms and three dining rooms at the inn.

Set on ten acres in the heart of Virginia hunt country, the inn is modeled after small inns in the south of France. Guestrooms are individually decorated in French decor, and some have fireplaces. Guests may relax on the spacious porch or terrace with a glass of wine. Or they may opt to enroll in one of Alain's French cooking classes at the inn.

Canoeing, horseback riding, golfing, and touring vineyards are all nearby. Guests may opt to have the inn pack a special picnic basket and enjoy several parks and scenic drives in the area.

L'Auberge Provençale
P.O. Box 119
White Post, VA 22663
703-837-1375

Pear Almond Muffins

These muffins often accompany an artfully-displayed gourmet entree that Master Chef Alain Borel creates to please his guests. Makes 28 muffins.

 3 ripe pears
 2 tablespoons almond extract
 ½ cup water
 2¼ cups flour
 ¼ teaspoon baking powder
 2 teaspoons baking soda
 1 teaspoon salt
 2 cups sugar
 3 eggs
 1 cup oil

- Preheat oven to 350 degrees. Spray muffin cups with nonstick cooking spray.
- Peel and core pears. Purée pears in a blender with the almond extract and water until smooth.
- Sift together the flour, baking powder, baking soda, and salt. Set aside.
- In a mixer bowl, mix the sugar, eggs, and oil. When well mixed, add the flour mixture, blending well. Pour in the pear mixture slowly, blending well until pear mixture is all incorporated.
- Fill each muffin cup ¾ full.
- Bake for 18 to 20 minutes. Serve warm with butter and jams, or just as they are.

The Lamplighter Bed & Breakfast

*J*udy and Heinz Bertram and their cocker spaniel, Freddy, welcome recreational and business travelers to their Queen Anne-style home, which was built in 1895 by a local doctor as his home and office. After living for more than twenty years in Germany and traveling extensively throughout Europe, the Bertrams brought their collection of fine antiques and original paintings and lithographs to their Michigan B&B.

They purchased their "dream B&B" virtually overnight, Judy said. She and Heinz added a deck with a gazebo and a red brick patio and extensive landscaping so that summer guests can enjoy refreshments outside. Judy is a Michigan native and former administrator in the Department of Defense school system overseas, and Heinz, originally from Germany, is a retired U.S. Air Force officer.

Breakfast may be served on the patio, in the gazebo or in the formal dining room, depending on the season. Afterwards, guests might head off to swim in Lake Michigan, stroll along its miles of sandy beaches, walk to the lighthouse at the entrance to Ludington harbor, or shop for antiques. Guests find plenty of outdoor activities year 'round, including biking through Ludington State Park, rated one of the state's best, skiing on miles of groomed cross-country trails, or hiking or strolling along nature trails. Judy and Heinz are happy to help guests plan their itinerary to explore scenic Western Michigan.

The Lamplighter Bed & Breakfast
602 East Ludington Avenue
Ludington, MI 49431
Toll-free 800-301-9792
Fax 616-845-6070

Pineapple Cream Muffins

"These are wonderful muffins that kids and adults alike will gobble up," writes Judy Bertram. "If there are leftovers, refrigerate them in a covered container and serve them cold — they're even better!" Makes 15 muffins.

- 2 cups flour
- 2 teaspoons baking powder
- ½ teaspoon baking soda
- 3½ ounces instant vanilla pudding
- ⅔ cups brown sugar
- 1 egg, beaten
- 1 cup sour cream (regular or low-fat)
- 1 8-ounce can crushed pineapple, with juice
- ½ cup oil

- Preheat oven to 425 degrees. Spray muffin cups with nonstick cooking spray.
- In a large bowl, sift together the flour, baking powder, baking soda, pudding mix, and stir in brown sugar.
- In a separate bowl, combine the egg and sour cream. Fold in the pineapple and oil. Add the egg-pineapple mixture to the flour mixture, stirring until moistened. Batter will be thick.
- Bake for 15 minutes.

Grünberg Haus Bed & Breakfast

*I*n the early 1970s, George and Irene Ballschneider closed their New Jersey delicatessen and headed to Waterbury, Vermont. For five years, they cleared a space in the forest and hand-built an inn they'd designed from memories of their travels in Austria. Armed only with a hammer and a saw, George rose at 5:00 in the morning each day. Irene collected furnishings, sewed curtains, and stenciled furniture for every room in the inn, all the while raising three children. When the Schneider Haus opened to guests in 1972, George and Irene became the area's favorite hosts. After 12 years, the couple retired to Florida, and the inn fell into disrepair under its new owners.

In 1988, Mark Frohman and Chris Sellers drove up the inn's driveway on a snowy November night and discovered the Tyrolean-style inn that would become their new project. Under a new name, which means Green Mountain House, the first guests arrived in June 1989 — just after Mark had disconnected the septic system to rebuild it. As renovations proceeded, Chris organized concerts, craft fairs, and Octoberfests at the inn. In 1994 and 1995, Mark built three cabins up in the woods behind the inn and a carriage house suite to provide a variety of lodging options.

Each of the Grünberg Haus' ten romantic guest rooms is eclectically furnished with comforters, quilts, and antiques. All rooms open onto a carved wood balcony with views of the Green Mountains and a path leads back to a whirlpool tub set in the woods. Breakfasts are events: While Mark serves guests at a table overlooking the mountains, Chris entertains quietly at the grand piano in the background. Vermont maple syrup and cheeses are featured in recipes such as maple-poached pears and ricotta-stuffed French toast.

Grünberg Haus Bed & Breakfast
Rural Route 2, Box 1595
Waterbury, VT 05676
802-244-7726
Toll-free 800-800-7760

Pumpkin Apple Streusel Muffins

"I've seen guests tuck a few of these dense, rich muffins in the pockets of their jackets for munching later on the ski lifts," writes Innkeeper Chris Sellers. Makes 18 muffins.

2½ cups flour
2 cups sugar
1 tablespoon pumpkin pie spice
1 teaspoon baking soda
½ teaspoon salt
2 eggs
1 cup canned pumpkin
½ cup oil
2 cups McIntosh apples, chopped

Streusel Topping
4 teaspoons butter
¼ cup sugar
½ teaspoon cinnamon

- Preheat oven to 350 degrees. Grease muffin cups.
- Combine flour, sugar, pumpkin pie spice, baking soda, and salt.
- In a separate bowl, combine the eggs, canned pumpkin, oil, and chopped apples; mix with the flour mixture just until moistened.
- Scoop batter into greased muffin cups.
- To make topping, cut together butter, sugar, and cinnamon until crumbly; top muffin batter evenly.
- Bake for 30 to 35 minutes.

Lord Mayor's
Bed & Breakfast Inn

*T*his elegant Edwardian house was the home of the first mayor of Long Beach, Charles H. Windham. His unofficial Edwardian-style title, Lord Mayor, was bestowed by British beauty contestants enjoying the amenities of this seaside resort in the mid-1900s. The Lord Mayor's house was meticulously restored by historians Reuben and Laura Brasser and received the prestigious 1992 Great American Home Award from the National Trust for Historic Preservation for sensitivity in restoration of a historic house.

Located in the heart of Long Beach, Lord Mayor's Inn is close to many major businesses, shopping, dining, and leisure activities. Within walking distance are city and state government offices, the World Trade Center, the Promenade, Farmers Market, and the Blue Line rapid transit.

Gracious hospitality awaits guests in the Brassers' home. These innkeepers have a reputation for friendliness and fabulous food. Enjoy coffee in the kitchen, a scrumptious breakfast in the dining room or outdoors in the fresh sea air on one of the porches.

There are five spacious bedrooms upstairs. All bedrooms have access to a sun deck. The bedrooms' decors differ, as do the beds. Try the Eastlake Room decorated in Eastlake Design; the four-poster bed in Beppe's Room; the Hawaiian Room with its hand-carved bed; the original master bedroom with its own fireplace; or the room that was originally used by Mayor Windham's daughter, with its twin eighteenth-century Austrian beds.

Lord Mayor's
Bed & Breakfast Inn
435 Cedar Avenue
Long Beach, CA 90802
310-436-0324

Pumpkin Spice Muffins

Tasty, moist, golden brown, and with a heavenly baking aroma, these muffins are low-fat to boot! "They are delicious any time of the year," said Innkeeper Laura Brasser. "Guests enjoy these with whipped cream-topped fruit compote. They freeze well, and the recipe may be doubled." Makes 12 muffins.

2 cups cake flour
½ cup sugar
½ teaspoon baking soda
½ teaspoon baking powder
½ teaspoon salt
½ teaspoon cinnamon
½ teaspoon nutmeg
½ teaspoon ground cloves
1 cup canned pumpkin
½ cup low-fat buttermilk
1 egg
2 tablespoons oil

- Preheat oven to 375 degrees. Line muffin pan with paper liners.
- Combine the flour, sugar, baking soda, baking powder, salt, cinnamon, nutmeg, and cloves, and stir well.
- In another bowl, whisk the pumpkin, buttermilk, egg, and oil together until smooth. Gently fold the pumpkin mixture into the flour mixture, being careful not to overmix.
- Bake for about 25 minutes or until deep golden brown on the tops. Cool slightly and serve immediately.

Thimbleberry Inn
Bed & Breakfast

*T*his new contemporary home, opened as a bed-and-breakfast in May 1993, features 375 feet of Lake Superior frontage and has a spectacular view of five of the Apostle Islands. The three guestrooms each have a private entrance and a working fireplace. Guests enjoy freshly brewed gourmet coffee and homemade muffins delivered to their rooms in Longaberger baskets a half hour prior to a full gourmet breakfast. Breakfast is served on the spacious deck, weather permitting, or in the dining area overlooking the islands. Innkeeper Sharon Locey loves cooking. She has entered and won several prizes in dairy bake-offs, has taught 4H food classes and a holiday foods class for two colleges, and is a field editor for a popular cooking magazine.

Thimbleberry Inn is located just south of Schooner Bay on Lake Superior. Its lovely wooded setting offers guests a quiet secluded getaway in which to walk among the trees on the forty-acre property or along the lake, or just relax in an outdoor Adirondack love seat and enjoy the restful sound of the waves lapping against the shore. Guests may be fortunate enough to see one of several eagles that soar along the lake shore. For the more adventuresome, the inn recently acquired a sailboat, and offer half-day and full-day trips among the Apostles. Bayfield is home to the Apostle Islands National Lakeshore.

Thimbleberry Inn
Bed & Breakfast
15021 Pageant Road
P.O. Box 1007
Bayfield, WI 54814
715-779-5757

Raisin Bran Muffins

"Feel free to halve this recipe," says Innkeeper Sharon Locey. She makes up the whole batch and stores the batter, ready to bake in the morning, covered in the refrigerator for up to six weeks. Fresh-baked muffins were never easier! Makes about 48 muffins.

> 5 cups flour
> 3 cups sugar
> 5 teaspoons baking soda
> 1½ teaspoons salt
> 7½ cups (1 15-ounce box) raisin bran cereal
> 4 cups buttermilk
> 1 cup vegetable oil
> 4 eggs, beaten
> butter, melted, optional
> cinnamon-sugar mixture, optional

- Preheat oven to 400 degrees. Lightly grease muffin cups.
- Blend flour, sugar, baking soda, and salt in a large mixing bowl. Stir in cereal.
- Add the buttermilk, oil, and eggs, and blend until dry ingredients are moistened. Do not stir batter again. (Mixture may be stored, covered, in a nonmetal bowl in the refrigerator for up to 6 weeks.)
- As needed, fill muffin cups ⅔ full.
- If desired, lightly brush melted butter over the batter, and sprinkle with cinnamon sugar before baking.
- Bake for 15 to 20 minutes.

The Woods House
Bed & Breakfast

*I*n the spring of 1991, Françoise and Lester Roddy moved from Berkeley, California, and purchased the Woods House Bed-and-Breakfast Inn, which has been in existence since 1984. Françoise previously worked in human resources and event planning, and brought calligraphy, cooking, needlecraft, and gardening skills to the innkeeping business; Lester brought over 25 years of business management. Both innkeepers enjoy creating taste treats for their guests, such as fresh peach pie. The Roddys also enjoy setting up theme weekends. The inn hosts popular "murder mystery weekends" at Valentine's Day, Halloween, and New Year's Eve; and in the spring and fall, they host workshops for aspiring innkeepers.

The Woods' half acre of terraced English gardens is shaded by majestic trees and abounds with flowers and herbs and quiet places for guests to relax. The 1908 Craftsman-style inn has six guestrooms, and is just four and one-half blocks from the downtown plaza.

The Woods House Bed & Breakfast
333 North Main Street
Ashland, OR 97520
541-488-1598
Fax 541-482-8027

Raspberry Cornmeal Muffins

Innkeeper Françoise Roddy describes these muffins as "a moist and tender cornbread with the pleasant surprise of fresh red raspberries." Her guests gobble them up! Makes 12 muffins.

- 1 cup cornmeal
- 1 cup unbleached flour
- ½ teaspoon salt
- ½ cup brown sugar, packed
- 1 teaspoon baking powder
- ½ teaspoon baking soda
- 1 egg
- ¼ cup butter, melted
- ½ cup buttermilk
- ½ cup orange juice
- 1 cup fresh or frozen raspberries (if frozen, do not totally defrost the berries)

- Preheat oven to 400 degrees. Line muffin pan with paper liners, and spray top of pan with nonstick cooking spray.
- Combine the cornmeal, flour, salt, brown sugar, baking powder, and baking soda.
- In a separate bowl, combine the egg, butter, buttermilk, and orange juice. Beat well. Add the flour mixture to the egg mixture, stirring just to combine. Add the berries; do not overmix.
- Fill the muffin cups ¾ full.
- Bake for 15 to 20 minutes.

Just-N-Trails Country Inn

A third-generation dairy farm, the Just-N-Trails Country Inn property has been in the Justin family since 1914. In 1985, Don and Donna Justin opened ten kilometers of cross-country ski trails, and the B&B opened a year later. The award-winning Just-N-Trails is set among the scenic wooded hills and valleys of southwestern Wisconsin, near Sparta. The cozy 1920s farmhouse with four guestrooms is complemented by three private luxury cottages: the Granary, the Little House on the Prairie, and the Paul Bunyan — the last two are log cabins.

Donna treats her guests, hungry from the previous day's worth outdoor activities, to a four-course breakfast that features homemade muffins, granola, yogurt, applesauce or fresh fruit, an entrée, and of course coffee, tea, and juice. Area attractions include 12½ kilometers of private, groomed cross-country ski trails, snowtubing, snowshoeing, hiking, biking on the Elroy-Sparta Trail, canoeing, and visiting the nearby Amish community, state and national parks and forests, and quaint antique shops. Guests are encouraged to play with the rabbits, kittens, Peter the pygmy goat, and chickens on this working farm. Donna also notes that they serve dinner on Friday and Saturday nights, and they can accommodate meetings, parties, and reunions for up to 35 people.

Just-N-Trails Country Inn
7452 Kathryn Avenue
Sparta, WI 54656
608-269-4522
Fax 608-269-3280

Rhubarb Pecan Muffins

Even guests who aren't normally rhubarb-lovers fall for these muffins. Innkeeper Donna Justin serves them as soon as the rhubarb is ready for cutting in the spring. Makes 24 muffins.

- 4 cups flour
- 3 teaspoons baking powder
- 2 teaspoons salt
- 1½ cups sugar
- 1 teaspoon baking soda
- 2 eggs
- 2 teaspoons orange rind, grated
- ½ cup oil
- 1½ cups orange juice
- 2½ cups rhubarb, finely chopped
- 1½ cups pecans, ground

Glaze
- ¼ cup orange juice
- ½ cup sugar

- Preheat oven to 375 degrees. Line muffin pan with paper liners.
- Measure flour, baking powder, salt, sugar, and baking soda into a large mixing bowl. Stir.
- In a separate bowl, beat the eggs, and add the orange rind, oil, orange juice, rhubarb, and pecans.
- Add the egg-rhubarb mixture to the flour mixture, stirring until just combined.
- Using an ice cream scoop, place the batter into muffin cups.
- Bake for 20 minutes, or until browned on top.
- For the glaze, combine the orange juice and sugar, and let sit while the muffins are baking. Cool the muffins slightly, and dip the tops into the orange juice mixture.

Angel Arbor
Bed & Breakfast Inn

*V*eteran Houston Innkeeper Marguerite Swanson, with her husband, Dean, opened Angel Arbor Bed-and-Breakfast Inn in September 1995 after a busy six-month restoration. Marguerite successfully operated Durham House B&B Inn, just a half-block away, for ten years before "downsizing" to this slightly-smaller Georgian-style home. Both homes were once owned by Jay L. Durham, a Houston Heights benefactor. As father of seven, he aspired to acquire a house for each of his children, but fell short of that goal because of the Great Depression.

Marguerite, a San Antonio native, easily moved into innkeeping as a profession. "I came from a big family and I was used to entertaining, and I just loved the idea of having people in my house all the time," she said. "I never have a day when I wake up and wish I were doing something else." Durham House quickly established a reputation for gracious accommodations and special occasions, such as unique murder mystery dinners, teas, showers, and small private parties.

In order to have a little more free time, she and Dean bought the elegant red brick residence that is now the Angel Arbor. It has four spacious guestrooms upstairs. The 1923 home, built for Katherine and John McTighe, had most recently been used for offices. The Swansons removed glued-down carpet, refinished the original hardwood floors, installed new bathrooms, and replaced many residential fixtures. They turned the screened porch into a year-round solarium, which overlooks the garden, with Marguerite's favorite angel statue and Dean's favorite vine-covered arbor. Guests are welcome to enjoy the garden, as well as the first-floor parlor, solarium, sunroom, and dining room.

Angel Arbor Bed & Breakfast Inn
848 Heights Boulevard
Houston, TX 77007
713-868-4654
Toll-free 800-722-8788

Spicy Peach Muffins

Moist and delicious, these muffins are one of Innkeeper Marguerite Swanson's favorites because they can be made from ingredients easily on hand year-round. And guests love the heavenly aroma of these muffins baking. Makes 12 muffins.

2	cups flour
½	cup sugar
2	teaspoons baking powder
1	teaspoon baking soda
½	teaspoon salt
1	teaspoon cinnamon
½	teaspoon nutmeg
dash	mace
1	egg
⅓	cup oil
⅓	cup milk
1	8-ounce carton peach yogurt
½	cup dried peaches, finely chopped

Topping

2	tablespoons sugar
½	teaspoon cinnamon

- Preheat oven to 400 degrees. Grease muffin cups.
- Combine the flour, sugar, baking powder, baking soda, salt, cinnamon, nutmeg, and mace in a large bowl.
- In a separate bowl, combine the egg, oil, milk, yogurt, and dried peaches. Add the egg mixture to the flour mixture, stirring just until the dry ingredients are moistened.
- To make topping, combine the 2 tablespoons sugar with the ½ teaspoon cinnamon.
- Spoon into greased muffin cups. Sprinkle the top of each muffin with the cinnamon-sugar.
- Bake for 20 minutes, or until toothpick inserted in middle comes out clean. Do not overbake.

The Beazley House
Bed & Breakfast Inn

*J*im and Carol Beazley gave up careers — he was a photojournalist and she a registered nurse — to open Beazley House in 1981 as Napa's first bed-and-breakfast inn. "Some of our friends thought we were nuts," says Carol, "but the only thing we were afraid of was not getting the chance to try." The mansion they found is in old Napa, just a stroll from shopping and fine restaurants. Napa is only an hour north of San Francisco at the southern gateway of the world-famous Napa Valley wine country. It is a tree-shaded, river city surrounded by vineyards and wineries. Within minutes of the inn are wine touring, ballooning, cycling, hot mud baths, and mineral spas.

The Beazley House sits on half an acre of lawns and gardens. Visitors will see why it has been a Napa landmark since 1902 with its verdant lawns and bright flowers and welcoming stained glass front door. Elegant yet comfortable, the sitting room is to the left, and the beautiful gardens can be seen through the French doors straight ahead. The guestrooms are large and individually decorated with beautiful antiques and queen-sized beds. The Carriage House, nestled among gardens and tall trees behind the mansion, is the "country side" of the inn. In it, five charming, generous rooms with private spas and fireplaces await guests' discovery.

For breakfast, Beazley House serves a delicious buffet of fresh-baked muffins, crustless quiche, a variety of fresh fruits with yogurt, sweet orange juice, and a selection of teas and steaming coffee. Innkeepers Jim and Carol Beazley specialize in tasty, low-fat cuisine that pleases their guests.

The Beazley House
Bed & Breakfast Inn
1910 First Street
Napa, CA 94559
707-257-1649

Strawberry Shortcake Muffins

What could be better than strawberry shortcake for breakfast? Innkeepers Carol and Jim Beazley have replicated that dessert treat in a low-fat muffin that they can serve all year long. Makes 36 muffins.

6 cups flour
1 cup sugar
1 ½ tablespoons baking powder
1 ½ tablespoons baking soda
3 cups frozen, unsweetened strawberries, chopped (not thawed)
3 cups low-fat buttermilk
3 eggs
3 egg whites
3 tablespoons oil
sugar

- Preheat oven to 350 degrees. Spray muffin cups with nonstick cooking spray.
- In a large bowl, combine the flour, sugar, baking powder, and baking soda. Mix the frozen strawberries in with the flour, and stir until berries are just coated.
- In a separate bowl, combine buttermilk, eggs, egg whites, and oil. Combine buttermilk mixture with flour-strawberry mixture. Do not overmix.
- Fill each muffin cup about ¾ full with batter. Sprinkle about ¼ teaspoon of sugar on top of each.
- Bake for about 15 to 20 minutes.

Old Rittenhouse Inn

*A*n Upper Midwestern landmark that has been featured in numerous national publications, the Old Rittenhouse Inn attracts guests to this picturesque harbor town with its elegant regional cuisine and luxurious overnight lodging.

Musicians-turned-innkeepers, Mary and Jerry Phillips bought this three-story hilltop mansion in 1973 and opened a country inn long before the bed-and-breakfast "industry" was born in the Midwest. As Mary's talents as a chef blossomed, the Rittenhouse became known for its gourmet cuisine, as well as its charm and hospitality. The main inn, an 1890 Queen Anne Victorian, was built as a summer cottage for General Alan C. Fuller of Belvedere, Illinois. The Phillips have decorated the rooms with their collection of period antiques and grand wall coverings.

To accommodate visitors, the Old Rittenhouse Inn is now made up of four historic Bayfield landmarks with a total of 21 guestrooms, including the newly-opened Fountain Cottage. Guests gather at the main inn for meals. The Rittenhouse features a five-course gourmet dinner in the evening, which may include Lake Superior smoked trout salad, Bayfield apple-glazed pork chops, or other local favorites, as well as homemade breads, preserves, and desserts. Bayfield has a wonderful supply of fresh raspberries and apples, in season, as well as Lake Superior trout and whitefish, of which the inn takes full advantage.

Chosen by the readers of *Wisconsin Trails* magazine as having the best breakfast in the state, the Rittenhouse's first course fruits and oven-fresh bakery allow guests to experience the changing of the seasons. The entrée course may include such favorites as Wisconsin herb scramble or wild rice pancakes, accompanied by crisp apple-cured bacon or spicy chorizo lamb sausage.

Old Rittenhouse Inn

301 Rittenhouse Avenue
Bayfield, WI 54814
715-779-5111
Fax 715-779-5887

White Chocolate Muffins

"As a lover of fine white chocolate, I can hardly think of a sweeter way to wake up and face the day than with this warm, fragrant muffin, with its delicate surprise in the center," said Innkeeper Jerry Phillips. "This recipe is special to me because it is one which Mary and I developed together through the various stages of testing and tasting." Makes 12 muffins.

  1 egg
 ¼ cup oil
 ¾ white chocolate liqueur
 ½ cup milk
 ½ teaspoon almond extract
  2 cups flour
 ¼ cup sugar
  2 tablespoons baking powder
 ⅓ cup white chocolate, grated
 ¼ cup sliced almonds, toasted
 12 ½-inch chunks of white chocolate

- Preheat oven to 325 degrees. Grease muffin cups.
- Combine the egg, oil, white chocolate liqueur, milk, and almond extract. Mix well.
- In a large bowl, combine the flour, sugar, baking powder, grated white chocolate, and toasted almonds. Make a well in the center, and add the egg mixture. Stir just enough to blend.
- Fill muffin cups ½ full. Add 1 chocolate chunk to each muffin. Add more batter to fill the cups ¾ full.
- Bake for about 15 minutes.

Angel Arbor
Bed & Breakfast Inn

*V*eteran Houston Innkeeper Marguerite Swanson, with her husband, Dean, opened Angel Arbor Bed-and-Breakfast Inn in September 1995 after a busy six-month restoration. Marguerite successfully operated Durham House B&B Inn, just a half-block away, for ten years before "downsizing" to this slightly-smaller Georgian-style home. Both homes were once owned by Jay L. Durham, a Houston Heights benefactor. As father of seven, he aspired to acquire a house for each of his children, but fell short of that goal because of the Great Depression.

Marguerite, a San Antonio native, easily moved into innkeeping as a profession. "I came from a big family and I was used to entertaining, and I just loved the idea of having people in my house all the time," she said. "I never have a day when I wake up and wish I were doing something else." Durham House quickly established a reputation for gracious accommodations and special occasions, such as unique murder mystery dinners, teas, showers, and small private parties.

In order to have a little more free time, she and Dean bought the elegant red brick residence that is now the Angel Arbor. It has four spacious guestrooms upstairs. The 1923 home, built for Katherine and John McTighe, had most recently been used for offices. The Swansons removed glued-down carpet, refinished the original hardwood floors, installed new bathrooms, and replaced many residential fixtures. They turned the screened porch into a year-round solarium, which overlooks the garden, with Marguerite's favorite angel statue and Dean's favorite vine-covered arbor. Guests are welcome to enjoy the garden, as well as the first-floor parlor, solarium, sunroom, and dining room.

Angel Arbor Bed & Breakfast Inn
848 Heights Boulevard
Houston, TX 77007
713-868-4654
Toll-free 800-722-8788

Zucchini Lemon Muffins

"These are very lemony and tangy because of the fact that I don't think zucchini has any taste by itself!" notes Innkeeper Marguerite Swanson. Her guests are often surprised to find this delicious muffin has a vegetable baked into it. Makes 12 muffins.

    2 cups flour
    ¾ cup sugar
    1 tablespoon baking powder
    ½ teaspoon salt
       grated rind of 1 lemon
    ½ teaspoon nutmeg
    ½ cup pecans or walnuts, chopped
    2 eggs
    ½ cup milk
    ⅓ cup oil
    1 teaspoon lemon extract
  1 ½ cups zucchini, shredded

- Preheat oven to 400 degrees. Grease muffin cups.
- In a large bowl, mix flour, sugar, baking powder, salt, lemon rind, and nutmeg. Stir in the nuts.
- In a small bowl, beat the eggs slightly. Beat in milk, oil, and lemon extract. Add the egg mixture to the flour mixture, and stir in the shredded zucchini just until blended.
- Bake for 20 minutes, or until toothpick inserted in middle comes out clean.

ARIZONA
Graham Bed & Breakfast Inn, The; Sedona, AZ — *Banana Pistachio Muffins (21)*
Peppertrees Bed & Breakfast Inn; Tucson, AZ — *Bacon Cheese Muffins (19),*
Chili Cheese Corn Muffins (37)

CALIFORNIA
Beazley House Bed & Breakfast Inn, The; Napa, CA — *Mandarin Orange Muffins (81),*
Strawberry Shortcake Muffins (121)
Daly Inn; Eureka, CA — *Cran-Blackberry Muffins (53)*
Inn at Shallow Creek Farm, The; Orland, CA — *Elderberry Muffins (63)*
Old Thyme Inn; Half Moon Bay, CA — *Cranberry Orange Muffins (51)*
Lord Mayor's Bed & Breakfast Inn; Long Beach, CA — *Pumpkin Spice Muffins (111)*
Rancho San Gregorio; San Gregorio, CA — *Double Chocolate Muffins (61)*

COLORADO
Holden House 1902 Bed & Breakfast Inn; Colorado Springs, CO —
Blueberry Corn Muffins (27)
Black Dog Inn; Estes Park, CO — *Chocolate Mint Muffins (41)*

DELAWARE
Wild Swan Inn; Lewes, DE — *Peach of a Tomato Muffins (101)*

FLORIDA
Hoyt House Bed & Breakfast; Fernandina Beach, FL — *Cream Cheese Breakfast Cakes (55)*

MAINE
Old Iron Inn Bed & Breakfast, The; Caribou, ME — *Chocolate Cheesecake Muffins (39)*
Red Shutters; York Beach, ME — *Orange Chocolate Chip Muffins (89)*

MASSACHUSETTS
Allen House Victorian Inn; Amherst, MA — *Orange Pumpkin Nut Muffins (95)*
Diantha's Garden Bed & Breakfast; Southampton, MA — *Key Lime Muffins (79)*

MICHIGAN
Inn at Ludington, The; Ludington, MI —
Jane's Double-Good Michigan Blueberry Muffins (77)
Lamplighter Bed & Breakfast, The; Ludington, MI — *Almond Muffins (7),*
Pineapple Cream Muffins (107)

MINNESOTA
Lady Goodwood Bed & Breakfast, The; Stillwater, MN — *Grandmother's*
Strawberry Muffins (73)
Park Row Bed & Breakfast; St. Peter, MN — *Apple-Barb Muffins (9)*

MISSOURI
Garth Woodside Mansion Bed & Breakfast Country Inn; Hannibal, MO — *Orange*
Marmalade Muffins (91)
Doanleigh Inn, The; Kansas City, MO — *Butterscotch Oatmeal Muffins (31)*
Walnut Street Inn; Springfield, MO — *Ozark Persimmon Muffins (97)*

MONTANA
Good Medicine Lodge; Whitefish, MT — *Melba Muffins (85)*

NEW HAMPSHIRE

Apple Gate Bed & Breakfast; Peterborough, NH — *Apple Carrot Cinnamon Muffins (11)*
Buttonwood Inn, The; North Conway, NH — *Coconut Muffins (45)*
Inn at Maplewood Farm, The; Hillsborough, NH — *Maplewood Nut Muffins (83)*
Watch Hill Bed & Breakfast; Center Harbor, NH — *Harvest Fruit Muffins (75)*
Windyledge Bed & Breakfast; Hopkinton, NH — *Peach Cobbler Muffins (99)*

NEW MEXICO

Grant Corner Inn; Santa Fe, NM — *Peanut Butter Bran Muffins (103)*

OHIO

Grandma's House Bed & Breakfast; Orrville, OH — *Apricot White Chocolate Muffins (17)*

OREGON

Woods House Bed & Breakfast, The; Ashland, OR — *Ginger Rhubarb Muffins (67),*
Raspberry Cornmeal Muffins (115)

PENNSYLVANIA

Wedgwood Inns; New Hope, PA — *Applesauce Raisin Muffins (15), Glazed*
Lemon Blueberry Yogurt Muffins (69)

TENNESSEE

Adams Hilborne; Chattanooga, TN — *Glazed Raspberry Lime Muffins (71)*

TEXAS

Angel Arbor Bed & Breakfast Inn; Houston, TX — *Banana Walnut Whole-Wheat*
Muffins (23), Spicy Peach Muffins (119), Zucchini Lemon Muffins (125)
Bonnynook Inn, The; Waxahachie, TX — *Brandied Apple Morning Muffins (29)*
Delforge Place, The; Fredericksburg, TX — *Date Nut Muffins (57)*
McCallum House, The; Austin, TX — *Cocoa Banana Muffins (43)*

VERMONT

Grünberg Haus Bed & Breakfast; Waterbury, VT — *Pumpkin Apple Streusel Muffins (109)*
Inn at the Round Barn Farm, The; Waitsfield, VT — *Morning Glory Muffins (87)*

VIRGINIA

Inn at Gristmill Square; Warm Springs, VA — *Orange Nut Muffins (93)*
Fairlea Farm Bed & Breakfast; Washington, VA — *Cranberry Cream Cheese Muffins (49)*
L'Auberge Provençale; White Post, VA — *Pear Almond Muffins (105)*

WASHINGTON

Salisbury House; Seattle, WA — *Ginger Pear Muffins (65)*

WISCONSIN

Inn at Cedar Crossing; Sturgeon Bay, WI — *Carrot Bran Muffins (35), Door County*
Cherry Almond Muffins (59)
Just-N-Trails Country Inn; Sparta, WI — *Rhubarb Pecan Muffins (117), Craisin*
Chocolate Chip Muffins (47)
Old Rittenhouse Inn; Bayfield, WI — *White Chocolate Muffins (123)*
Stout Trout Bed & Breakfast, The; Springbrook, WI — *Apple Crunch Muffins (13),*
Caramel Pecan Upside-Down Muffins (33)
Thimbleberry Inn; Bayfield, WI — *Raisin Bran Muffins (113)*
Victorian Treasure Bed & Breakfast Inn; Lodi, WI — *Black Bottom Muffins (25)*

Ordering Information

Order additional copies of any of our popular B&B cookbook editions from your bookstore, gift shop, or by mail.

Innkeepers' Best Muffins *and* **Innkeepers' Best Low-Fat Breakfast Recipes** *are the first in a series of practical one-topic cookbooks showcasing bed-and-breakfast innkeepers' outstanding recipes. Each 6 x 9–inch paperback retails for $9.95 ($12.95 each by 4th class mail; $13.95 each UPS ground service).*

WAKE UP & SMELL THE COFFEE *is a series of hefty 8 ½ x 11–inch softcover cookbooks that feature travel information, maps, an index, as well as more than ten chapters of breakfast, brunch, and other favorite fare from B&Bs in a particular region.*

> **Lake States Edition** *has 203 recipes from 125 B&Bs in Michigan, Wisconsin, and Michigan: $15.95 ($18.95 by 4th class mail; $19.95 UPS ground service).*
> **Southwest Edition** *boasts more than 170 recipes from 65 B&Bs in Texas, Arizona, and New Mexico: $14.95 ($17.95 each by 4th class mail, $18.95 each sent UPS).*
> **Pacific Northwest Edition** *features more than 130 recipes from 58 B&Bs in Washington and Oregon: $11.95 ($14.95 each by 4th class mail, $15.95 each sent UPS).*

Look for **WAKE UP & SMELL THE COFFEE's Northern New England Edition** *(Maine, Vermont, and New Hampshire), and* **Chocolate for Breakfast and Tea,** *coming soon!*

TO ORDER BY MAIL, send a check to Down to Earth Publications, 1032 W. Montana, St. Paul, MN 55117. Make checks payable to Down to Earth Publications. MN residents please add 7% sales tax. **TO ORDER WITH VISA OR MASTERCARD,** call us at 800-585-6211.

Mail to: Down to Earth Publications, 1032 W. Montana, St. Paul, MN 55117.

Please send me:

> _____ *Innkeepers' Best **Muffins***
> _____ *Innkeepers' Best **Low-Fat Breakfasts***
> _____ *WAKE UP & SMELL THE COFFEE — **Pacific Northwest Edition***
> _____ *WAKE UP & SMELL THE COFFEE — **Lake States Edition***
> _____ *WAKE UP & SMELL THE COFFEE — **Southwest Edition***

I have enclosed $_____ for _____ book(s). Send it/them to (no P.O. boxes for UPS):

Name: _____

Street: _____ Apt. No. _____

City: _____ State: _____ Zip: _____
    (Please note: No P.O. Boxes for UPS delivery)